The
POWER of
PRESENCE

The
POWER of
PRESENCE

Unlock Your Potential to Influence and Engage Others

KRISTI HEDGES

American Management Association

New York · Atlanta · Brussels · Chicago · Mexico City
San Francisco · Shanghai · Tokyo · Toronto · Washington, D.C.

Bulk discounts available. For details visit:
www.amacombooks.org/go/specialsales
Or contact special sales:
Phone: 800-250-5308
E-mail: specialsls@amanet.org
View all the AMACOM titles at: www.amacombooks.org

This publication is designed to provide accurate and authoritative information in regard to the subject matter covered. It is sold with the understanding that the publisher is not engaged in rendering legal, accounting, or other professional service. If legal advice or other expert assistance is required, the services of a competent professional person should be sought.

Author's Note: All case studies are based on actual clients; however, in order to protect client confidentiality, names and details have been changed unless specificially called out by full name or company. In general, case studies are composites of multiple persons to be most illustrative of the author's point.

Library of Congress Cataloging-in-Publication Data

Hedges, Kristi.
    The power of presence : unlock your potential to influence and engage others / Kristi Hedges.
        p.   cm.
    Includes bibliographical references and index.
    ISBN-13: 978-0-8144-1773-7 (hardcover)
    ISBN-13: 978-0-8144-3785-8 (paperback)
    ISBN-13: 978-0-8144-3786-5 (e-book)
        1. Executive ability—Psychological aspects.   2. Leadership—Psychological aspects.
    3. Self-presentation.   4. Influence (Psychology)   I. Title.
    HD38.2.H43   2012
     658.4'09—dc23

                                                                                    2011026474

About AMA
American Management Association (www.amanet.org) is a world leader in talent development, advancing the skills of individuals to drive business success. Our mission is to support the goals of individuals and organizations through a complete range of products and services, including classroom and virtual seminars, webcasts, webinars, podcasts, conferences, corporate and government solutions, business books, and research. AMA's approach to improving performance combines experiential learning—learning through doing—with opportunities for ongoing professional growth at every step of one's career journey.

Printing number

10 9 8 7 6 5 4 3 2 1

FOR SMITH AND EMERY, my joy

AND FOR MY HUSBAND, MIKE,
my partner in everything

Contents

Preface

We're all experts at presence. I study it. You do too. Presence has many descriptions. We may call it confidence, or charisma, or being compelling—but we experience it the same. When we meet someone with a strong presence, we can feel it. And if the person is a leader, we are inspired by it.

Executive presence is the corporate "it" factor.

We are constantly assessing people in a variety of settings based on their presence. It is important to us because presence is a neon sign announcing who people are. Often, whether we decide to work with someone boils down to the individual's executive presence.

Executive presence is multidimensional and dynamic. It means much more than being a great public speaker or making a fantastic first impression. It's about impressions made over time. Executive presence doesn't relegate itself to one segment of our professional lives. People who have a strong presence are able to connect with and inspire those around them across situations. That is never more important than when you need people to follow your lead through a period of uncertainty and change—precisely what today's leaders at all levels must do every day.

> *Executive presence means much more than making a fantastic first impression. It's about impressions made over time.*

Like many things a person cares deeply about, my own personal interest with presence started when I was a kid growing up in a small town in West Virginia in the 1970s. Like most southern towns, my hometown had a clear line between social classes. My family was squarely working class, where people found jobs that simply paid the bills and a manufacturing position was considered top shelf. There was unstated yet palpable pressure to observe your station in life. Anyone seeming to rise above his class got called out for putting on airs. *Who does he think he is?* None of this came with malice. It just was.

I noticed at a young age how people carried themselves, especially when speaking with someone considered in a class above them. The first tactic was avoidance. Adults from different classes never mixed socially. Social power dynamics were visceral. You could almost see the intimidation exude from someone in conversation with a social superior. Growing up, I heard many discussions about how "one of them" demeaned "one of us" in a required exchange. No one questioned the authority of a person in a position of power. And forget about asking a lot of questions of your doctor. It just didn't happen.

My grandmother was a different sort. I watched her carry herself through the world and make things happen. She was a small woman weighing only about 98 pounds, yet she had tremendous stature. She spoke to everyone, rich or poor, with confidence and dignity. She was always impeccably dressed, wearing a suit and heels most days, well into her 80s. People gravitated to her. She had a core group of friends her entire life. Her presence gave her power far beyond those around her, and everyone wanted to be near her, including me.

She had an amazing impact on me growing up. She instilled a sense of worth in me, advising me to walk tall, hold my head up, and look people square in the eye. She showed me how to talk to anyone as an equal. All of this motivated me to do better for myself—and my way out was education. I was a straight-A student all through school, which put me in classes with students mainly from professional families. I was always the poorest kid in the bunch. My life experience was embarrassingly small. I had never traveled more than a few hours from my hometown until I went away to college. To move in those circles all I had was my own presence. I figured out that no one has absolute confidence, but we

No one has absolute confidence. You just need to find a seed of confidence to create an environment where your full confidence can grow.

have enough to get us started if we dig deep. And that seed creates an environment where your full confidence can grow.

Fast-forward to my final year at Virginia Tech, when I was nominated to be the outstanding senior for the entire college of Arts and Sciences, which graduates 800+ students each year. It was a huge honor. I was a communications major going up against the hard sciences and math scholars, you name it. The final three candidates were interviewed by a panel of judges for qualities of academic excellence, leadership, and community service. When I went in for the interview, I was riddled with nerves. All I could do was call on my presence—even if it was just a seed—to display confidence, excitement, and passion. I was told that my interview was the deciding factor. I won the award and was the first person from my department to receive that honor.

For graduate school I won a full scholarship to Purdue University, a top-five communications program known for deep social science research. There I pieced together a master's program for myself around power in communications. I studied what made political candidates electable. I made it a lifelong pursuit to uncover the secret of presence because I knew the impact it had. I spent the first part of my career in politics, helping federal candidates get elected to office. When I entered the field, which runs on relationships and connections, I knew absolutely no one. All I had was my presence. I managed to get in front of the right people and built a network one person at a time. Looking back, sometimes I can't believe I pulled it off.

Presence is the great equalizer. That's true not just for me growing up, but for anyone in a professional situation. Presence has the power to bring people to you, and to open any door. I've relearned that power repeatedly throughout my career. I've leaned on my presence to work my way through corporate environments, strike out as an entrepreneur before the age of 30, manage a business through volatile markets, and reinvent myself a few times along the way. Not only does this confidence create presence, but more important, presence can create confidence. Today, in my job as an executive coach and leadership consultant, I work with people eager to have a more powerful presence. The concept of presence is nebulous for most people. They know it when they see it in others but are unsure of how to get it themselves. There's a mystique about presence that suggests a person just has it, and perhaps people are born with it.

Executive presence is frequently misunderstood. Most often I hear it referred to as showmanship, or having the commanding presence of a titan of industry, even as you struggle with your first managerial position. In fact, executive presence doesn't necessarily translate into being a fantastic presenter or showman, though that may be a powerful by-product. And it's not exuding unabashed confidence regardless of the circumstances.

This book dispels myths about presence. It shines a light on what presence actually is and how it can be cultivated. I'll show you why and how anyone, regardless of personality type, can strengthen their presence. It works for introverts as well as extroverts; it works without regard to position or level of power. And best of all, it has nothing to do with becoming someone you're not; rather, it's about being more of who you already are.

Executive Presence That's for Everyone

Some people wonder, "What if I'm a professional but don't consider myself an executive per se, or don't aspire to the corner office? What if I'm a community leader, team manager, or entrepreneur?" I use the phrase *executive presence* because that's the term most frequently used in business today. It conjures an image of confidence that we readily visualize. The concepts behind executive presence are exactly the same as those behind leadership presence, personal presence, or, simply, presence—and I use the terms interchangeably throughout the book. Keep in mind that although the ideas are presented within a business context, they will benefit you in all aspects of your life.

If You Want a Game Changer, This Book Is for You

I was driven to write this book because executive presence as a corporate requirement is reaching a fevered pitch. It is frequently showing up in performance reviews, and people routinely are getting hired, fired, and promoted based on it. Organizations are bringing in coaches (like me) to help leaders cultivate it. Presence has become one of the key differentiators—and a critical success factor—for professionals today.

And that makes sense. In a world where we have all become

free agents who must constantly maintain our personal brand, differentiation is what it's all about. Years of experience and service won't prevent you from being downsized. Good performance alone won't get you the promotion you want. Tried-and-true sales tactics feel stale when prospects can go online for any information they seek to make their buying decisions. Markets change on the whim of a college kid's competitive idea, and leaders must adjust themselves and their people just as quickly. And if the most recent market downturn has taught younger workers anything, it's that even a degree from an Ivy League school doesn't guarantee you a job.

But a stronger presence can benefit anyone. Your presence can be your professional Midas touch. This book shows you how to use your presence to stand out and be the kind of person others clamor to work with—and how to do it in a way that feels natural and authentic to you. You'll find this book especially helpful if you are:

— An executive trying to create a market-leading company
— A leader who must set a vision and galvanize others
— A manager of employees trying to increase or turn around performance
— A professional positioning for a promotion or new position
— An executive looking to rebrand yourself or change careers
— A job seeker interviewing for a new position

The game has changed. Powerful executive presence will be your personal game changer.

The
POWER of *PRESENCE*

Introduction

For 20 years, presence has been not just my profession but also my passion. And it's been a winding path that's led me here.

In my career, I've been the person behind the leader. I've worn a few different hats: CEO coach, entrepreneur, public relations executive, corporate marketer, and political consultant. In each role, I've been privy to what goes on with leaders as they struggle to motivate, inspire, and impress audiences as small as one and as large as one million. I've seen the anxiety, heard the lack of confidence, throttled back runaway egos, and managed the stage fright.

Somewhere along the line I also became a leader, running my own company and being the one out in front. Because I've used my own techniques and advice on myself, I understand what succeeds and what falls short.

Politics, where I started my career, is an interesting training ground for leadership. In that world, a candidate's presence is always top of mind. It's discussed, polled about, massaged, and widely known to be the make-or-break factor. (Think Hillary Clinton in her 2008 run for president: Countless polls were taken and articles written about her inability to connect with voters and be likable. Democratic insiders worried it was her Achilles' heel. It wasn't until she showed her humanness by breaking down during an interview that her likability increased, as did her poll numbers.) Political strategists know that we connect individually with our leaders first, and only then can we grant the trust to give them our vote. A candidate's background is scoured for personal stories with which voters can connect— stories that break down perceived barriers between the candidate and constituents.

When I had the opportunity to segue into public relations, I took this experience from politics into the corporate world. In traditional public relations, the focus is 90 percent on the message and only 10 percent on the messenger. So I bit my tongue a lot in the beginning as I watched beautifully messaged speeches decimated by a CEO whose body language screamed, "I don't totally believe what I'm saying!" But the engine that fuels the PR world is content, and time and money is spent on developing stronger messages, writing press releases, and, nowadays, blogging and participating in social media.

The Secret Life of Struggling Communicators

As I made my way into the inner sanctums of companies as a PR consultant, I found that a leader's presence is often considered to be personal—something that is not discussed. Eventually, I started my own communications firm and worked with hundreds of CEOs and leaders as a trusted adviser. Routinely, a company official would whisper that the CEO was a poor communicator or lacked presence. No one wanted to deal with it head-on. Time-consuming and expensive workarounds were often employed, such as having paid spokespersons or keeping the CEO behind the scenes. At most, we could gain agreement for media training or a good speechwriter. Everyone knew that while those solutions helped, something was still lacking.

Other times, I had the opportunity to tackle the issue directly with the CEO. I found that most leaders cared deeply about their own presence and how it affected their leadership ability. My clients' communication challenges took different forms: Some leaders were confident with their ability to communicate one-on-one, but not in groups. Others had a hard time connecting with individual executives, and many feared speaking in public. Because the idea of presence seemed like something that should come with a leader's title, people were embarrassed by the shortcoming. It caused anxiety. I've met more than one CEO who relied on Ambien to combat the sleepless nights leading up to a board meeting or important presentation, and who then popped a Xanax to get through it.

Because people think presence should come with a leader's title, they are often too embarrassed by the shortcoming to address it.

I began developing tools to give my clients a process and structure to improve their presence. This skill building produced results, because my clients steadily improved their effectiveness. Yet often the results were hard-won or fleeting. As I learned years later, there was more to the story.

Concurrent with my work with leaders, my own experience as a leader was unfolding. I started my first company, one of the first Washington, D.C.-based technology PR firms, at age 28. In less than two years, my business partner and I grew the business from a two-person shop into a well-known agency with dozens of staff members and millions of dollars in revenues. We developed a reputation as a go-to agency for creating technology brands, with a focus on smart strategies and deep customer relationships. Our name got around so quickly that we turned away more business than we accepted—and we still had a three-month backlog! Within six months of opening our doors came the first of several acquisition offers. We experienced great success helping our clients achieve greatness, with front-row seats taking companies public or through industry-defining mergers and acquisitions that turned them into global brands.

On the rare occasions when I could slow down, it was only to feel a mix of disbelief and pride for what we had created from pure tenacity. We had succeeded beyond my wildest dreams. I was honored as one of the top PR professionals in the country under the age of 35 and named a leading businesswoman in Washington, D.C. Our firm took its place as one of the largest independent agencies and women-owned businesses in the D.C. area. That tenacity came in handy later, as the technology bubble burst, 9/11 happened, and we learned to navigate historically tough market conditions. You learn twice as much on the way down as you do on the way up—and in the 10 years I had the firm, we had a few rides both ways.

Behind the scenes of those accomplishments, I faced a steep, seemingly endless learning curve. I was young and terribly inexperienced in leadership when we founded the firm, so I fumbled through a lot of situations where what was required of me surpassed my knowledge and ability. I used presence techniques on myself as I simultaneously developed them for clients. For me, the outside work with clients and business development came naturally, but I struggled with being the internal leader. I read leadership books, took courses, and joined a CEO development group. I failed a lot. I succeeded some, too. There were times I nailed my goal of inspirational and connected leadership. Keeping our team together and catapulting our company into a market-leader position, despite considerable market odds post-9/11, were huge personal accomplishments.

Then there were other times when the daily stresses of running a business and managing staff issues overwhelmed me. My intentions and my words were out of alignment, and everybody knew it. Frustration undercut my capability. Everyone—employees, clients, industry peers, media, lawyers, and advisers—seemed to need the best piece of me. Mental exhaustion was common from the pressure of having to be "on" in each interaction. I tried to learn from my mistakes and experiences as I went. My proudest moments were when my team members reached out to thank me for being a mentor, or used their experiences to go out and build even more success in their careers. That was my impetus to keep working on my own leadership presence.

A decade after I cofounded the company, I sold my share and became a leadership coach. I took some time to reflect and question what I knew to be true in my work with leaders. What is it about some people who can get others to follow with ease? What qualities do they possess that engender trust? How can presence be learned if one's own skills aren't enough? Why did I personally experience so much inconsistency?

As a coach, I began working with my clients' thought patterns, preconceptions, and mental focus—their "inner" presence. I also developed an interest in neuroleadership, a burgeoning field that marries leadership with brain science and the study of human behavior. It offers some remarkable findings about why people have a hard time changing and sustaining new behaviors.

Over the course of several years, I refined my approach and saw powerful, lasting shifts for clients. Through this experience I developed I-Presence, a model that I have found to be the "secret sauce" of executive presence. It is equal parts communication aptitude, mental attitude, and authentic style. It combines a supportive inner mindset with the outer skills needed to create the natural, confident, consistent leadership presence we all seek.

The I-Presence Model to Inspire and Motivate Others

This book takes you through the three-step model of I-Presence (Figure I-1) and provides easy-to-use tools, exercises, and strategies to integrate the concepts into your everyday work. Some of these concepts will be new to you, while you may be familiar with others.

I've laid out the model in step form so that the concepts become actions. And because we learn so well from the stories of others, you'll also find examples of leaders who can demonstrate behaviors that impact presence. Furthermore, because we all struggle with so many of the same issues, I've included numerous case studies of executives—developed as composites from leaders I've observed and worked with over the years—so you can see how others in your situation have managed.

> *Give yourself permission to be more of yourself, rather than less.*

My goals are to get you to reorient your beliefs about what makes a strong executive presence and rid yourself of limiting behaviors, while providing you with new ways of thinking *and* doing.

I-Presence is at once intentional, individual, and inspirational.

Figure I-1.   The I-Presence Model.

Intentional
Your beliefs shape every aspect of your presence, from body language to the actions you choose to undertake. Therefore it is critical to get your head around what type of presence you want to demonstrate, the values you want to convey, and how that matches up (or doesn't) with how others currently perceive you. The first part of this book describes how to become more aware of your own presence and impact, and then provides useful tools for creating alignment between your intentions and how you want to be perceived.

Individual
We connect with individuals, not with the hierarchical concept of a leader or manager. Whether with employees, customers, investors,

or the market at large, these connections drive business, loyalty, and career success. And counter to what you may believe, building these connections doesn't involve having all the right answers or working harder than everyone else. In this part of the book, I'll uncover the relationship-building secrets of successful leaders and the ways in which you, too, can form deep connections with others and build relationships that foster trust.

Inspirational

What tools are in your toolkit when you want to inspire others? What's the best way to address a group and get people excited? What do powerful communicators do that's different? This final part of this book outlines the specific communication techniques that will improve your outer presence. I'll cover a range of must-have executive presence skills, including powerful language, employee and team communications, motivating through change, visionary leadership, gaining eminence, and high-impact presenting to senior management, boards, employees, and public audiences of all sizes.

A Little Presence Goes a Long Way (or Leadership for the Overwhelmed)

Perhaps you've already read a lot of leadership theory. New ideas always sound compelling, but if you are like me, you become overwhelmed because you can't do everything. This book is designed to help you focus on and leverage your greatest potential as a leader— your own presence. It challenges you to be more of yourself, rather than less.

And here's the best part: Because your presence is integral to everything you do, even if you choose to work on only one lesson learned from this book you will have a positive result. I've written the book to make it easy for you to select concepts that resonate with you by including short takeaways at the end of each chapter, as well as leaving room for you to jot down ideas to try as you go.

Read on, figure out what works for you, and get the ball rolling.

PART 1

INTENTIONAL

Understanding and Managing
Your Presence of Mind

CHAPTER 1

What Are You Thinking?

Executive presence begins in your head. It resides in how you think about yourself, your abilities, your environment, and your potential.

Nearly everyone has an excellent presence; it may simply manifest itself in another part of your life. Perhaps you are charismatic and confident as your son's baseball coach, or you are empathetic and inspiring to your best friend. You give a bang-up speech at your college friend's 40th birthday party, or have just the right words to encourage your sister.

Most of what you need is right there in you, waiting to be tapped for your professional life.

If you are concerned that having executive presence means faking it, consider yourself reassured. The kind of presence that attracts other people to you, makes your team want to move mountains for you, and propels you ahead is the opposite of fake. It is pure authenticity—being more of the person you already are, without the mental subterfuge that gets in the way.

Intentionality is the driver of presence. All the communication tips in the world won't make up for your thought patterns.

I-Presence starts with "intentional" presence, because it is the driver. There are no tips or tricks that will make up for a lack of intentionality. In fact, sometimes tips can make things worse. Many executives, fresh from tip-laden training in public speaking, find themselves even more nervous and less authentic than before because it feels forced. They have all the same feelings and anxieties about speech giving, but now they are also trying to remember to stand this way or gesticulate that way. You can buy an expensive car with all the latest features and a GPS, but if you don't know the address of your destination, you won't get where you want to go.

You need to pick up the right intentions and let go of what's in the way.

Intentional Is as Intentional Is Perceived

You may be thinking, "Isn't every functioning professional intentional? If I weren't, I couldn't keep my job." Well, yes, you're right. And I bet you can point to many times in your day when you aren't as thoughtful about your actions as you could be—especially as it relates to your presence. And we can easily call out this tendency in other people, too.

Let me take a moment to describe what I mean by being intentional: I define having an intentional presence as understanding how you want to be perceived and subsequently communicating in a manner so that you will be perceived the way you want. It means aligning your thoughts with your words and actions. And it requires a keen understanding of your true, authentic self, as well as your impact on others.

There are different kinds of intentions. Some are broad and relatively stable, such as when you declare, "I want to be a visionary leader." Other intentions are situational, such as, "In this strategy session, I must be the catalyst for change." We'll discuss various types of intentions in the chapters in Part 1, and how to put them into practice in your life.

Trust that intentions change your presence. I see it every day. You will, too.

You Are What You Think, Even When You're Not Paying Attention

In January 2001, *Harvard Business Review* featured an article by Jim Loehr and Tony Schwartz labeling today's executives as corporate athletes.[1] The article addressed how to bring an athletic training methodology to the development of leaders. This approach makes tremendous sense on a number of levels, and especially in terms of mental conditioning.

Anyone who follows sports knows the importance of an athlete's focus. We all admired Michael Phelps at the Beijing 2008 Olympics as he listened to his iPod stone-faced, concentrating, before he dove into the water. We respect an athlete's ability to use positive visualization and intention, and readily acknowledge its benefit.

Somehow, though, outside of athletics such rituals seem unnecessary or even silly. It reminds us of Al Franken's famous *Saturday Night Live* character Stuart Smalley saying to himself in the mirror, "I'm good enough, I'm smart enough, and doggone it, people like me." Taking the time to have the discussion with yourself about what you want to accomplish with your presence may seem more like pop psychology/self-help than hard-core executive training.

Guess again. Taking the time to figure out what you want your presence to convey is a critical and powerful first step. That is the image of yourself you want to keep in mind as you do your own dive into the water. It's your mental aim.

The Wrong Internal Conversation: Why I'm a Disaster at Golf (and You Might Be, Too)

As you develop your mental aim, you also need to determine what conversation is currently in your head and how it may need to change. Even when you aren't paying attention, your internal conversation is always happening.

Scott Eblin, author of *The Next Level,* convincingly describes intention as a "swing thought," likening it to the last thing golfers think before their club strikes the ball.[2] (Eblin is a coaching colleague from Georgetown, and I have to thank him for the original comparison of intention to athletic focus—a common reference that's helpful for so many people to think about.)

For anyone who has played golf, you readily get the swing-thought idea. And even if you haven't, you can probably understand how hitting that tiny ball dead-solid perfect requires a whole lot of mental focus. It's the make-or-break factor.

When I was in my early thirties, I decided to learn golf. I took lessons, got the right clubs, and practiced diligently. At the driving range with the pro, I wasn't half bad. However, I was terrible when I got on the course. Competitive and averse to failure, I was self-conscious about how I played compared to others around me. I'd choke when I got to the tee and have an all-around miserable game. When I was paired with other golfers, it got even worse. Still I kept trying, remaining furious at myself for hitting well in practice and then falling apart on the course. After a few years with no improvement, I gave it up.

My golf-playing days were before I was a coach. At the time, I didn't have the ability to fully understand what was happening. When I got up to the tee, my swing thought was literally, "Don't embarrass yourself." Is it any wonder that I was such a disaster?

Negative swing thoughts are alive and well off the golf course. I hear them from clients all the time, either stated or unstated. They include:

— I can't speak in public.
— I'm not a people person.
— I'll appear self-promoting.
— I'm an introvert and can't network well.
— I'm just not good in these situations.
— I don't have what it takes to play the office politics game.

Any of these pretexts sound familiar? If this is where you are placing your mental focus, you can bet it's showing up in your presence, and maybe even screaming.

Neuroleadership is discussed in-depth in Chapter 9. One of the main findings of those studying in this field is that our intentions actually shape how the human brain functions. The intentions that we hold in our head, either positive or negative, create mental shortcuts that become a veritable path of least resistance. The more we think something, the easier it is for our mind to process it. That's why it's critical to be fully aware of any negative thoughts blocking your progress. I've included an exercise (see sidebar) to help you "uncover your negative thoughts."

> *The intentions we hold in our head create mental shortcuts that become a path of least resistance.*

Uncover Your Negative Thoughts

Find a quiet space to contemplate what you believe to be true about your presence. Write down any negative thoughts that may hold you back.

- What do you currently think about your own executive presence and your ability to affect it?
- What assumption of yours is getting in the way or holding you back, and why? How long have you felt this about yourself?
- Try on the idea that you already possess the presence you seek in the various areas of your life. What's your reaction?

Knowing what our limiting thoughts are, and replacing them intentionally, is the only way to create a different possibility. Eventually, the possibility becomes the new and improved shortcut.

How Intention Plays in the Course of Work

A few years ago, I was coaching Alan S., a senior executive at a Fortune 500 finance company. He was frustrated because he felt that with his experience and background, he should be perceived as a high-performer with the C-suite in his grasp. Yet he was passed over for a promotion. Believing his communication style might be to blame, Alan hired me as his executive coach to work on it.

As I do with most engagements, I started out by speaking with Alan's colleagues to get an accurate picture of how he was perceived by other people. (See Chapter 4 for how to conduct your own presence audit.) Their take was that Alan was rarely positive about other people's suggestions. They felt that since he was overly critical, it was best to avoid him. He had great skills, they said, but it was easier to stay clear of him than to solicit his help. Who had the time in a busy day to be dragged down?

At first, Alan bristled at this feedback. He thought of himself as a pragmatist, but overall a positive person. After we delved into his thinking patterns, it became clear that more often than not, his pragmatism caused him to look for what could go wrong in a situation. Only after debunking every negative would he entertain any positive. We also assessed situations where he had face time with his colleagues and corporate officers: executive team meetings. Because there were so many voices competing during meetings, he tended to hang in the back of the room because he didn't see his contribution as additive (pragmatism again). When I asked what his thoughts were in the meetings, he realized his internal dialogue was, "Don't say anything stupid." Sometimes he even scowled without knowing it, either in reaction to a comment or his own thoughts.

Not surprisingly, Alan was unintentionally making an impression, even though he believed that being in the background would keep him from making one. As I came to learn, he was actually a very caring person, but most of his colleagues didn't venture close enough to learn that about him.

After diagnosing what wasn't working, we began to create some new intentions that felt right to Alan. To develop them, we looked at leaders he respected and wanted to emulate, both inside the company and in his personal life. He stated a personal intention that he wanted to be seen as capable, positive, and helpful—someone his colleagues actively sought out. Next, we began determining when his stated intention counteracted his actions. One was obvious: He needed to smile more. He also made a conscious decision to hold back reservations when others brought ideas to him; in fact, he would even encourage what was good about their suggestions. He began to drop by people's offices, just to talk or offer help. And he completely changed his role in executive team meetings by sitting near the middle of the room and making a point to contribute something encouraging in every session.

An intentional presence creates the desired emotional reaction in others.

We used the exercise shown in Figure 1-1 to recognize and change Alan's intentions. This may be a good starting point for you as well to begin noticing how intention plays in your life.

For one week, notice what you are thinking right before you enter situations where you need to be on your game or want to have a powerful impact. Is your mental aim constructive or destructive?	Determine what you would like for your presence to communicate, such as confidence, capability, integrity, patience, etc.	For the second week, try on this new thought before each of the same meetings. What changes do you see?

Figure 1-1. Exercise to Observe Intention.

Great Intentions Create Great Reactions

Executive presence at its core is about creating an impression on others. You want your presence to propel you ahead in your work life by getting your desired reaction. Every day is a bombardment of opportunities to persuade, influence, motivate, attract, or inspire others.

Being intentional about your presence means that you must play in the realm of emotions. Humans are emotional beings, and we process information on emotional terms. Think about how you take in the presence of other people. They create an emotional reaction in you. It could be comfort, disdain, fear, excitement, or curiosity. If you think of your favorite boss or leader, you are very likely to conjure up emotional terms to describe that person.

With your presence, you are trying to marry your intent with another person's perception. This is where authenticity plays a big role. It's nearly impossible to make another person feel excitement, for example, if you aren't excited; likewise, you won't bring out someone else's confidence if you aren't confident. (Many of us have endured enough halfhearted corporate pep rallies to know how inauthentic they are.)

The Story of Steve and Stan: An Internet Sensation

Macworld 2007, the huge conference for Apple computer and electronics devotees, provides a perfect example and an unexpected
cautionary tale of a missed intention.

Each year, Macworld draws about 20,000 attendees fiercely
devoted to all things Apple and immersed in its unique culture set
by the late CEO Steve Jobs. It's also where Jobs delivers the
keynote debuting new Apple products and creating multimillion-
dollar buzz overnight. Jobs is known for his electric presenting
style. In video of the event, he takes the stage with a mix of humor,
excitement, authenticity, and just the right touch of mischief. In
his trademark black turtleneck, jeans, and sneakers, he looks
casual and relaxed. He talks to the audience as if they are old
friends swapping stories. You can sense the energy in the room lift
when he walks in. The audience can't wait to be inspired by the
visionary Steve Jobs.

Often, Jobs had other CEOs from partner companies join him
onstage. They knew what the audience expected. They matched his
enthusiastic tone and casual dress and understood that it was their
job to keep up the energy level. After all, part of Macworld is the experience of being caught up in—and identifying with—the excitement of the Apple brand. Apple equals cutting edge, and you're
cutting edge for being there.

A funny thing happened in 2007, the year Jobs revealed the first-
generation iPhone with Apple's distribution partner AT&T. As usual,
Jobs was magnetic. Unveiling the iPhone to a hushed crowd, he gar-
nered cheers as he described the functionality. The crowd was ripe
for more. Jobs introduced Stan Sigman, then CEO of Cingular,
AT&T's wireless division. When Sigman came onstage, it was apparent that he looked different: He was dressed in a polished suit more
appropriate for a boardroom than this conference hall with a rowdy
crowd at Macworld. Still, the audience gave him the benefit of the
doubt as he spoke enthusiastically, from the heart, about the first time
he saw the iPhone prototypes.

Then it all fell apart. Sigman reached in his pocket, brought out cue cards, and proceeded to read for seven of the longest minutes in the history of Macworld. His comments were disconnected and uninspired, sounding as though they came straight from the boilerplate of an AT&T press release. He looked physically stiff and uncomfortable. While we can't be sure that he didn't have an intention for his talk, he certainly didn't convey one. He overlooked the emotional reaction his presence should have had on the audience, and instead left everyone feeling bored, at best, and at worst, disappointed that Apple had picked such a dull partner.

The Stan Sigman experience became an Internet sensation immediately. Bloggers wrote about it, audience members posted comments, and journalists picked it up. YouTube videos went viral. He became the poster child for poor executive presence.

I show this video frequently in workshops where people are stunned that someone at Stan Sigman's level would present so badly. But it is about more than presentation skills. Sigman rose through the ranks of telecommunications and built a hugely successful company. He knows how to present. He failed to determine the emotion he wanted to impart and then set the intention that would inspire that emotion in others. His presence should have conveyed excitement, creativity, and innovation. If he had succeeded, 20,000 people would have been a lot happier. It was an anemic beginning, unbefitting a culture-changing product.

Build a Strong Intention (or How to Be More Steve than Stan)

Intention has the power to work for us or against us, so why not cultivate it for good? In this book I discuss cultivating two types of intention:

— Your personal presence brand
— Situational intentions

Taking the time to consider, develop, and use both kinds of intention have far-reaching implications for your presence.

Your Personal Presence Brand: The Big Intention

Your personal presence brand is what you want your presence to convey overall. It shows your core values and beliefs. It reflects your personality. Forward-looking and far-reaching, it is how you aspire to present yourself at work, and potentially in the rest of your life as well. Your personal presence brand is backed by your actions, which I discuss in detail in Chapter 2. Like any brand, your personal presence intention doesn't change on a whim. It's relatively static, building over time. Ideally, it's an internal touchstone, a reminder of how to present the best version of you.

The sidebar "Determine Your Personal Presence Brand" contains an exercise to help you cultivate yours.

|||||||||||||||||||||||||||||||||||||||||||||||||||||||||||||||||||||||||||||||||||||||||||||||||||||||||||||||||||||

Determine Your Personal Presence Brand

1. Fill out the following chart. Start with whichever column is easiest or go back and forth as necessary.

Qualities I admire/ value in others	What I want my presence to convey
_____	_____
_____	_____
_____	_____
_____	_____

2. Look at the column of qualities you want to convey and condense or rank them into a top 5 list.
3. Reflect on your list. What do these qualities have in common? Try to create a sound bite, acronym, or archetype for these qualities. For example, "Jack Welch of the education industry." Also abbreviate as much as possible: "Credible and Compelling; Visionary and Vocal—C2V2," or "Catalyst for innovation—CFI," or "Pinch hitter for critical programs." It can be anything you can keep in your thoughts—all that matters is that it has meaning and resonance for you.

|||||||||||||||||||||||||||||||||||||||||||||||||||||||||||||||||||||||||||||||||||||||||||||||||||||||||||||||||||||

Once you have your personal presence brand figured out, keep it top of mind. Post it on your desk or on your computer desktop if that helps. Return to it at times when you need to communicate strategically, exhibit presence, or even make an important decision. It is an always-available reminder of what you want to reinforce about yourself to others.

Your Situational Intention: "In the Moment" Calibrations

So, your personal presence brand—and the intentions that drive it—remains steady. But you are constantly calibrating your situational intentions depending on the circumstances at hand. And while situational intentions should build and never detract from your personal presence brand, different situations require different actions. A leader's personal presence brand may be "inspirational visionary," but that's going to be applied differently in a sales pitch than in a corporate meeting to announce a restructuring.

Your situational intention is about creating a desired impact. Rarely is it a one-size-fits-all scenario. I mentioned that people process information and events in emotional terms, and often this is a good place to focus your situational intention. Consider what emotion you want to invoke in your audience and you are generally close, if not spot on, to what your intention should be.

‖‖

Craft a Situational Intention

Before your next communications event, answer these questions:

1. How do you want your audience to feel about this exchange?
2. What emotion do you need to embody?

The answers to these two questions outline your situational intention. (Hint: Because you need to embody what you want to impart, the answers are generally the same.)

‖‖

The exercise I've outlined in the sidebar "Craft a Situational Intention" isn't the only approach that will work, but it is one of the most effective. Again, just as in the personal presence brand, it is less about specific verbiage or semantics and more about what creates the mind frame for you. A former workshop participant of mine once told me that she'd applied a situational intention of "We deserve to win!" and landed a multimillion-dollar client. You can't argue with that!

Now Try This: The Intentionality Frame

Typically, employees are most likely to interact with leaders at meetings. Meetings are, in fact, a fertile training ground to learn to use intentions effectively. And because of the repeated exposure (most meetings occur on a regular basis), the rewards are huge.

The types of meetings you attend (e.g., small groups, board meetings, sales calls) may be different depending on your position, but the dynamics are the same. Many of us overlook the importance of meetings. Some of us even approach them with disdain because they get in the way of "real" work. Actually, meetings are your best chance to make a positive impression on others. Learning how to contribute effectively, manage your points adeptly, and display confidence are part of moving up the ranks of any company. Careers are made (and waylaid) from interactions in meetings.

For many executives, meetings are also the places where important ideas are communicated and where other people assess their thought patterns and strategic ability. All eyes are watching—and determining what the person speaking is made of. Here's a tool called the Intentionality Frame to help you align your intentions to your contributions in meetings. The Intentionality Frame can be adapted to practically any situation.

Let's say, for example, that you need to have a meeting with an underperforming team that you supervise. You want to learn the root cause of the performance problem so that you can correct the issue. It helps if you have a personal presence brand you can reflect upon first. Then you know to set a situational intention for how you want to come across and what your presence needs to convey. For the sake of this discussion, let's make your situational intention "gravity with openness." Your situational intention goes in the center of the frame, as shown in Figure 1-2. Normally when we assemble the points we want to make, we do it either in our head or in

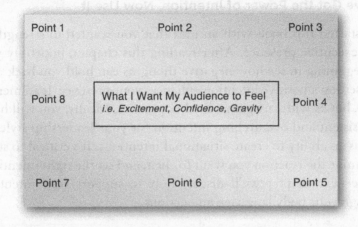

Figure 1-2. Intentionality Frame.

a vertical list. Instead, use the Intentionality Frame to make your points along the outer edge of the frame. If your intention is gravity with openness, your points around the frame might be (1) there's a clear issue though the cause is uncertain, (2) let's focus on solutions rather than blame, (3) it's important for everyone to commit to change from this meeting . . . and so on as you go around the frame. When you use this tool, your points stay in greater alignment with your intention. It's a visual trick—a mental reminder—to communicate your intention. You can also see that if your initial reaction were to start with some version of "If you don't improve performance, there'll be serious consequences," it would not support your intention. That's too heavy on gravity with no room for openness.

I often use the Intentionality Frame to help people have tough conversations. I start by having them write lists of points they want to make to the other person. Then they apply the Intentionality Frame. It's always amazing to me how much their points change! That's why this tool is useful for keeping conversations focused, on track, and close to the goal. Again, it demonstrates the power of intentions.

Meetings are a fertile training ground for trying intentional communications.

The Intentionality Frame can be used for public speaking, executive briefings, one-on-ones, and sales meetings—virtually any type of human interaction.

You've Got the Power of Intention, Now Use It

You started this book with an idea that you wanted to strengthen your executive presence. After reading this chapter, hopefully you are beginning to see how negative thoughts can hold you back and how setting a positive intention enhances your presence. It's a mental game, but as with any game, it takes practice. Ideally, you will have a consistent and overarching intention for your leadership style, as well as an ability to create situational intentions. It's critical to stop, determine the reaction you want to elicit, and set the right intention. In the next chapter we'll discuss how to support your intention through your body language and actions.

Key Takeaways from Chapter 1

1. Being intentional about your presence is similar to having an athlete's mental focus.
2. Uncover any negative thoughts you have about your presence that are getting in your way. Know what's playing just below your consciousness.
3. Set a positive intention for the kind of presence you want to convey overall. That's your personal presence brand. For inspiration, consider what leaders had an influence on you.
4. Set unique intentions for situations where you interact with others. Your intention should match the desired reaction from others, usually in emotional terms.
5. Use meetings as an effective training ground for establishing an intentional executive presence.

Ideas I Want to Try from Chapter 1:

_____

_____

_____

_____

_____

CHAPTER 2

Your Actions Are Speaking
So Loudly I Can Hardly Hear
What You're Saying

This chapter's title comes from an adage I read on a sign that a friend of mine used to keep on his desk. I always thought it was spot on. Our actions speak volumes, yet we spend scant time actually observing them. We're experts at reading *other* people's actions, and other people certainly know how to read ours. But how well can we read our own actions?

In the last chapter you learned how to set intentions for your presence. Now we'll cover how to ensure that your intention will be received with crystal-like clarity.

Our actions prove (or disprove) what we say about ourselves. They are signals for receivers to decode so that they can learn what we're all about. Actions can either *underline* or *undermine* our executive presence.

If you want to be seen as trusted and credible, then your actions must be in alignment with your intentions, both stated and unstated. It's the only way to be received with clarity.

Actions underline or undermine our executive presence.

All too often, we are unconscious of our own actions. This confuses our message; it can even make us seem as though we are misrepresenting ourselves. Especially in the workplace, when there is confusion, impressions quickly go to the negative. Have you ever known a colleague who promises to do something but fails to deliver? I bet it didn't take long to decide he was at best a B-player.

This chapter discusses how to understand your own actions and their impact on your presence. In terms of how people perceive and interpret you, two types of action are of equal importance:

— Micro-Actions (your body language, facial expressions, and tone of voice)
— Macro-Actions (how you spend your time, what you do, and your consistency)

Authenticity plays a key role here. My goal is not to make you an automaton with perfect body language and a personal schedule that is dictated by your presence objectives. My aim is to help you develop consistency and alignment. I want to make you aware of how to use your actions—your physical tools—to enhance the presence you feel at your core and want to convey to other people.

You have your intention. Consider your actions a megaphone. Make sure it's pointed in the right direction.

Body Language Is Important, but It Doesn't Buy Lunch

Everyone who has ever taken a course in public speaking knows that body language is key to effective communication in our personal and professional lives. And it *is* important. Don't get me wrong. But it's not the whole story.

In my work I've seen so much attention paid to the mechanics of body language that I've come to believe that it overshadows many other essential elements of communication. Everyone is looking for that power posture or commanding tone that will ensure success. I am routinely asked for the Right Way to stand, talk, gesture, or present. In fact, there is no Right Way. How you should stand, talk, gesture, or present depends on what you want to communicate. Anything else erodes authenticity—and for many people, confidence as well.

Because body language is a vehicle to get your message across, it should be in alignment with your message. If you want to convey openness, then clearly your body language can't suggest that you're closed off.

People have an intuitive sense about body language. In situations where we are comfortable, aligning body language with intention comes easily. The best way to improve your body language is to focus on your intention and make sure your body carries that message as well. (How you dress also counts as a form of nonverbal communication, with a similar need for alignment. See the sidebar for tips on how dress, as physical expression, can strengthen your presence.)

One of the reasons body language gets so much attention may be a misunderstanding about some significant research. Many readers of this book—especially anyone who has gone through corporate presentation training—may be aware of the relatively famous 55/38/7 rule. As it's usually discussed in popular culture, this rule says that when we communicate, 55 percent of our message is communicated through facial expressions, 38 percent through tone of voice, and only 7 percent through words. These statistics, explained in this way, have been used to scare the bejesus out of many, many people! "What if I don't have perfect body language?" you may be asking. "Will I totally bomb?" It's anxiety-inducing, to say the least.

And if you think about it a bit, it doesn't make sense. If I ask my husband to take out the garbage, he's not carefully reading my body language to determine what I *really* mean. Turns out, the statistics have been misapplied and distorted. They were originated by Albert Mehrabian, a professor of psychology at UCLA, and published in his book *Silent Messages* in 1981.[1] Mehrabian has tried on his own website to clear up the misinterpretation. He issues this delineation on his site about his omnipresent findings: "Please note that this and other equations regarding relative importance of verbal and nonverbal messages were derived from experiments dealing with communications of feelings and attitudes (i.e., like-dislike). Unless a communicator is talking about . . . feelings or attitudes, these equations are not applicable."[2] When we are trying to determine our feelings about someone, we rely on Mehrabian's filter. That's when body language plays a much greater role. It doesn't apply to all communications.

So words do matter, and perhaps nonverbal communication isn't a complete make-or-break factor. Take a deep breath on that one. There is an important learning here: In areas of persuasion, where we are trying to figure out if we trust someone, the importance of body language and tone plays a serious role. Take, for example, when a leader gets in front of the company to announce a new initiative. There's no doubt that how that leader carries herself during that message influences the group's buy-in. If her eye contact is sketchy and her tone of voice sounds shaky, the audience won't feel very sure, either.

Nonverbal communication is important, but it isn't always the make-or-break factor it's made out to be.

I bring up these points to further debunk the myth that your body language must be perfect. No one achieves that, and if you did, you wouldn't look genuine. Again, it's not about perfection, but about alignment.

Dress as Physical Expression: Is Your Self-Presentation Causing Dissonance?

There's a link between attire and presence, because how a person dresses is both a physical expression and a nonverbal communication. Dress is a factor in forming other people's impressions of us, and in this way, it impacts our presence directly. We may want to believe that corporate dress is about personal style only and shouldn't be a factor. When you consider the proliferation of makeover shows for men and women, you can see the power that clothing has over the way we view one another. (I once saw an episode of one such program where a tenured professor of nonverbal communication was made over. Her epiphany was that she'd been undermining her own credibility by not considering her self-presentation as a form of nonverbal expression. You can't make this stuff up. Our desire to believe dress doesn't matter is that strong.)

As a coach, I hear feedback that my client isn't polished, doesn't look CEO-like, or fails to exemplify a corporate officer. Many times, supervisors are delighted to share this feedback with a coach (especially one who specializes in presence) because they would never tell their colleagues themselves. Telling other people that they are inappropriately dressed is way too personal (not to mention it's potentially over the human resources line, especially when giving feedback to women). Attire has a real impact on careers. It's also one of the first aspects we notice about someone. It's a form of communication.

Yet, for many professionals, attire is fairly unintentional. The guidelines we use for selecting our clothes may be different from anything else in our professional lives. We may choose comfort over impression, for example, which would strike us as career-killing if we were talking about body language. Or we might not update our corporate wardrobe for years when we'd never let our functional skills atrophy for one month.

I'm not advocating for a right way to dress, just that it be *in alignment with your personal presence brand*. If you want to be creative and innovative, dressing like an Internet entrepreneur in funky suits and laid-back attire might be the way to go. If you are climbing the ladder at a Fortune 50 healthcare company and your intention is to be credible, you are better off dressing like the CEO, regardless of the corporate policy. Otherwise, you are creating some serious presence dissonance.

How you dress is just one of many aspects of your presence, but it's worth considering, especially if it doesn't cross your mind very often. Over the years I've seen, and heard, a lot of commentary around executive attire—most of it behind people's backs. Here are my best tips for dressing to strengthen presence, not detract from it:

- The adage to "dress for the job you want, not the job you have" always applies. Check out what the most senior executives wear for guidelines. Whenever you get promoted, your attire should be promoted as well—no exceptions.

- Keep your wardrobe updated. Styles change (yes, even men's suits), as do waistlines. At least once a year, add new pieces to your professional wardrobe.

- Make sure your clothes are properly fitted. It makes a tremendous difference. Department stores offer free personal shoppers (they even work during big store sales) who will find the right clothes for you and have them tailored on site. If you buy clothes online, factor in a trip to your local tailor before wearing.

- Don't dress for comfort; dress for presence. Casual Friday, or casual every day, does not mean sloppy. You can still look professional. There's a difference between dress jeans and washed-out jeans.

- Wear a jacket. A blazer goes a long way toward looking professional. It also allows you to dress up or down as needed during the day. (You can always keep one at work, too.)
- For women, never, ever wear revealing clothes at work. Even if you look fantastic in them, you won't be taken seriously.
- In general, the younger you are, the more conservatively you should dress. As you get more established in your career, you can add a bit more flair to your wardrobe because you have more gravitas. In your early years, you want to be taken seriously, and you don't have a lot of experience to back you up yet. Keep your wardrobe professionally nondescript.
- Anything connected to work counts as work. I'm talking about plane rides for business, retreats, even office happy hours or parties. The workplace rules still apply.
- Finally, think about your situational intention. What do you want your audience to think about you? Different audiences may require different attire. Dress like the group in front of you. If you don't know them well, dress more formally.

The discussion of attire is often avoided—yet never overlooked. Dress matters. I'm covering it because even if it isn't relevant to you, it may be to someone who works for you. Think of it this way: Dress is one aspect of your presence that you have complete control over, ahead of time. Dressing in a polished way, a bit above the mean, creates a positive impression and gets you noticed. So why not take advantage of it? And when all else fails, remember the words of Coco Chanel: "Dress shabbily, they notice the dress. Dress impeccably, they notice the woman." (This advice applies to non-dress-wearers too.)

|||||||||||||||||||||||||||||||||||||||||||||||||||||||||||||||||||||||||||||||||||||||||||||||||||||||||||||||||||||||||||||||||||||||

Present yourself in a way that underscores your intention. Take away some learning from the research. But the next time you hear it in a seminar, don't treat it as gospel. Remember that example of Steve Jobs from Chapter 1? Go on Apple's site and watch videos of his speeches. Jobs makes many body language "mistakes," if you believe what you read in books on public speaking. He paces. He tends to hold his arms too close to his body. He plays with things in his hands. But still he conveys the excitement and confidence that customers and shareholders adore. And the sum of his presence is legendary.

When You're Out of Alignment Your Body Knows It

In his book *Language and the Pursuit of Happiness,* author and executive coach Chalmers Brothers discusses the power of our internal thoughts and how they manifest themselves in our body language.[3] This is why having a positive intention has such an impact on how you embody your outward message. Brothers outlines an interesting exercise to show how your mind actually recognizes when your intention and your body language are out of alignment. I like to use it in this way: Sit in your chair with your worst body language on display. Sit slumped over, head down, frown on your face. Now, say something that you feel genuinely positive about in an upbeat voice, like, "I can't wait for my vacation to Italy." Notice what happens. Your body almost fights against the position. It feels wrong somehow and so inauthentic you may break out laughing. It's almost impossible to believe your own message! Your body language negates your words, and vice versa. (You can also do the reverse. Say something negative while sitting with great posture and a smile on your face.)

> *When you pay attention, you can sense your body language striving for alignment.*

When you pay attention, you can feel your body language striving for alignment. When you are relaxed, it flows. Unfortunately, in high-stress situations, you are anything but relaxed. I speak to large groups as part of my job, and still I have moments when I'm at a conference, ready to speak, and suddenly my heart starts racing. I've learned this about myself, so I make it a habit to practice my speeches out loud and with my full body. I want my muscle memory to kick in, so I can go back to my intention and my body language will follow. A first step to better body language: Know what you want it to look like so you can self-observe and self-correct as needed.

||||||||||||||||||||||||||||||||||||||||||||||||||||||||||||||||||||||||||||||||||||||||||||||||||||||||||||||||||||||||

Become a Body Language Researcher

1. Refer back to Chapter 1, to either the personal presence brand or a situational intention you wanted to set for your presence. Now think of a place in your life where this intention naturally occurs. For example, if your intention was "confidence," think about a time or place in your life—inside or outside of work—where you are comfortable and assured.

2. The next time you're in that situation, self-observe your body language in three areas: your face, gestures, and posture. (Think of it as a top-to-bottom, full-body scan.)

   • Face: Are you smiling? Are you making eye contact?

   • Gestures: Are your arms open or closed? Are your gestures large and wide or small and narrow? Where do your arms fall naturally?

   • Posture: Is your back straight or do you slouch? What is your stance? Do you walk, shift, or stay still?

3. Next, observe someone you admire in a similar situation. Consider those same aspects of body language—face, gestures, posture. How does the other person's body language measure against yours? What best practices can you create for yourself?

||||||||||||||||||||||||||||||||||||||||||||||||||||||||||||||||||||||||||||||||||||||||||||||||||||||||||||||||||||||||

The Science Behind Turning Your Frown Upside Down

When I was a freshman at Virginia Tech, walking across a crowded section of the campus between classes, I thought I was anonymous— just one in a sea of thousands of faces. Yet, on several occasions, guys would call to me: "Smile!" or "Lighten up!" or "Can it really be that bad?" Now given it was college, these guys didn't yet have fully developed social filters. They said whatever they felt. And their comments caught me off guard. For one thing, I wasn't unhappy in the slightest. I was just lost in my own thoughts about class, homework, or weekend plans. I had no idea I was frowning, let alone looking sullen enough to elicit a response.

Years later, when I was in the workforce and heard similar comments (only delivered more tactfully), I took the feedback to heart and literally looked in the mirror. I realized that my most relaxed expression is a frown. In other words, if I'm doing nothing I'm frowning. Not at all the presence I want to convey! So I worked hard to adjust my neutral expression to be upturned, or a slight smile. Now that expression feels natural to me. And thankfully, I no longer get cries to "lighten up."

This is a perfect example of consciously using body language to be more authentic. I'm not angry or frustrated. Most of the time, I'm grateful and happy. Now I make sure my true feelings are more visible.

I'm not alone in this example. I've talked to many clients and colleagues over the years who have had similar experiences of regularly being asked, out of the blue, "What's the matter?"

When clients see themselves on videotape, 99 percent say they need to smile more.

or being told they come across as intimidating. When I videotape clients and then show them their own presence, 99 percent of them say that they need to smile more.

There are two reasons that smiling warrants further discussion. First, we like when people appear happy. Smiles comfort us, elicit trust, and, frankly, just make us want to be around the person.

Of course, no one can smile all the time, and smiling can be inappropriate if it's out of alignment with your words. George W. Bush's ill-timed smirks earned him a spot in parodies for eight years. But in general, if you want to build a stronger presence, you have to be aware of how readily you smile.

The second reason is the circular effect of smiling. In his book *Blink,* Malcolm Gladwell mentions a research psychologist by the name of Paul Ekman, who is renowned for identifying and meticulously cataloguing thousands of human facial expressions. To undertake this enormous study, Ekman's team of researchers watched many hours of videotape that captured people's facial expressions and then imitated them to re-create specific muscular variations. During the study, an interesting side issue cropped up. Ekman found that when he and his team were making negative impressions, they tended to get depressed. So, like any good researcher, he tested his theory and found that in fact it was true. Expression by itself can make real changes in the autonomic nervous system. When we make negative facial expressions, we feel negative. And the reverse is true. We feel better when we smile. Gladwell explains Ekman's extensive research this way: "The face isn't a secondary billboard for internal feelings but an equal partner in the emotional process."[4]

Intrigued by Ekman's work, I interviewed him for my monthly leadership column at *Entrepreneur.com*.[5] He reiterated his findings about facial expressions and feelings. And he stressed that it is extremely hard to fake our facial expressions successfully. Ekman has identified micro-expressions that we all transmit but are so slight that they fly under our radar, so we are not even conscious of them. We can't fake them even if we try. (Professional poker players know this and compensate by wearing dark sunglasses.) That's why it's critical for people to be in touch with what they are trying to communicate, and to buy into it in a way that feels authentic to them.

So what does all this mean for your presence? First, smiling is one of the simplest micro-actions that builds an approachable and trustful presence. Unless you are delivering bad news, smiling is good. Second, smiling lifts your spirits in general, and feeling positive can only help you in your quest to build a stronger presence. Good feelings fuel confidence, which in turn fuels more good feelings. And finally, identifying, buying into, and keeping your intentions top of mind will help align your body language. When you are thinking "patience and positivity," those qualities are more likely to show up as such on your face—whether consciously or unconsciously.

Is Your Body Language Contagious?

Over the past decade, there has been a bevy of research on the subject of communication mirroring. Neuroscientists have discovered that our brains light up similarly to those with whom we're empathizing.[6] Some researchers also believe that our body language mirrors others naturally in trust situations. If you sit forward, I sit forward. If you frown, I frown. That's simply how we communicate empathy, and it's effortless. Body language is, in effect, contagious.

Consequently, like any good research, there's been a spate of ideas for how to apply it. For example, if mirroring works in close relationships, how do we use it to *form* close relationships? You can find many articles written about how to use mirroring purposefully to make other people more comfortable around us. I even attended sales training years ago that advocated sitting exactly the same way your clients do at the table and adopting their slang.

I don't know about you, but while an automatic brain function is one thing, strategic mirroring feels the opposite of authentic to me. I'm not going to advocate that you start mirroring everywhere you go. Instead, try the exercise in the sidebar titled "Become a Body Language Researcher" and once again recall your own natural body language in comfortable settings that reflected your intention. It's authentic to you and doesn't require the use of tricks to convince people that you feel empathy for them.

Your Red Blinking Light: Macro-Actions

Now that we've talked about how intentions play into body language, and vice versa, let's segue into your macro-actions, or how you spend your time. This includes where you show up or don't, what you produce or deliver, how consistent you are, and whether you keep your promises.

I regularly talk to CEO groups such as Vistage International, Entrepreneurs' Organization, and The Founder Institute. And I sit on the board of one called Mindshare. I love these groups because they are filled with ambitious, energetic entrepreneurs who care about their businesses. They are also frequently overextended from keeping a million balls in the air. They want to be better leaders, but they don't know how to focus their already-limited time. When I address these top executives, I introduce the concept of the red blinking light. When a leader walks into a room, it's as though a red blinking light is flashing a message: "This is important!" When the CEO goes into a meeting, the importance of that meeting rises. If he decides to skip a meeting, its importance is reduced. Leaders have to be keenly aware of not confusing their message by paying attention to where they spend their time. Because if the company message is, for example, "Sales is the top priority," and the CEO skips the big sales strategy session, it makes the message far less believable.

Confusing urgency with importance is another common and damaging problem for many leaders. If a leader tries to be everywhere all the time, then everything begins to look like a crisis, and nothing is deemed important. You can't be everywhere. So where should your red blinking light be today? This month? This year?

It's not just the CEO who has the red blinking light. Have you ever been at a company where a new initiative is announced? What does everyone do? They wait to see if there is any real movement by others in the company before they commit their own time and energy to the new idea. Until then, it's just words on a page.

The fact is that everyone carries around the red blinking light. All eyes go to our actions because they are the backbone of presence. We trust actions more than anything. Think about when we're first hired. People wait to see if we do what we promised in the interview. The first few months are critical because that's when everyone gets to see what we're made of. Even before that, recruiters make decisions partly on how candidates manage the interview process. Do they excel under pressure? Do they practice good follow-up? Are they meticulous with their preparation? And for those folks angling for a promotion, the top precursor by far is consistent performance over time.

When a leader walks into a room, it's as though a red blinking light is flashing a message: "This is important!"

Since we were kids, we've all heard that actions speak louder than words, right? It should be a moot point. But what happens is that real life steps in and we get busy. And that leads to a lot of unintentional actions. We take shortcuts. We put out fires. We let things slide and hope that no one will notice. Or we try to do everything and spread ourselves way too thin.

The red blinking light reminds us about being more intentional. For executives, it means committing to managing their actions as carefully as their words. For most people, it means you have to make choices about the actions you want to emphasize. The best place to start is by choosing the actions that make up your core values or, in other words, your personal presence brand.

Are You a McDonald's or a Starbucks?

When you developed your personal presence brand in Chapter 1, you determined what you want to be known for. To support this intention, you must also decide which actions to focus on the most. Your ability to give a reliable impression creates your image, just like a corporate brand. If McDonald's used unique ingredients and pricing in each of its restaurants, you'd have another feeling about the brand. McDonald's prides itself on providing a universal experience: similar restaurant design serving food that's fast, consistent, inexpensive, and pleases the masses. Starbucks creates a different yet equally reliable impression. It has built an amazing brand in a relatively short period of time by appealing to a subset of coffee drinkers who prefer a certain type of café experience. The company has made choices—good coffee, upscale pastries, green products— and that's where it never scrimps. The environment can be unique to the location, but you know what core products to expect when you walk in the door.

The client I mentioned in Chapter 1 wanted to be known as someone who was helpful—and he made that a core part of his brand. When there was an opportunity to assist a colleague by lending his expertise, he made sure to do it, even if it meant that other actions had to slide off his plate. And of course, people noticed that his actions underlined his presence. He used his red blinking light to create his personal presence brand.

In today's workplace, it is impossible to be 100 percent consistent about 100 percent of your actions. That's why we must choose. For CEOs, your personal presence brand may be exactly the same as the company's priorities. You are about integrity and so is the company. For professionals in other positions, or those in various stages of workplace (re)entry, your personal presence brand is individual. Perhaps you want to be known for efficiency, creativity, collaboration, or risk taking. Regardless, remember that your actions will underline or undermine your presence.

To help demonstrate this process, let me use a personal example of my own red blinking light, and how I used actions to support my brand. Having a personal presence brand of accountability is a deeply held core value of mine, which spans across my entire life and career. I'm chronically on time, will do almost anything to meet a deadline, and own up to my commitments probably far beyond what is expected of me. (This has a downside too, which rears its ugly head in my schedule.) When I get the sense that I'm shirking my duties or sloughing off work to someone else, I feel horrible. I don't give my word lightly, but when I do, I'm all in.

From my first job onward, this trait has meant that I'm frequently given the tough clients or the turnaround projects—a role that I relish most of the time because it plays to my strengths. In my early career, it even helped me develop a niche. No one likes to deal with difficult people, but turning them into happy customers is rewarding for me.

As a business owner with numerous employees and moving parts, dealing with heated client situations comes with the job. At times, your team gets called to the carpet for a misstep or misunderstanding and you're the best one to find a remedy. A veteran entrepreneur once told me that the owner can fix practically any problem a business faces, which was golden advice. Mistakes are inevitable, but how you deal with them makes all the difference. Nothing angers clients more than firms that refuse to acknowledge and accept responsibility for their share of the blame. We picked up many clients from such firms, as this is a common refrain. Again, accountability is my natural instinct, which is a plus. Yet, in the middle of a tough conversation it's hard to remain calm and positive without falling into defensiveness. Sometime the client *is* just difficult. In these situations, I have had to be carefully, even exquisitely, intentional to stay true to the brand I wanted to convey. I also needed to push back (gently) on issues that clearly weren't our fault to establish boundaries moving forward. Figure 2-1 lists the actions I intentionally took around client relations to underscore my desired brand as an accountable leader. Now, try this exercise: See if you can narrow down the actions you need to take on a daily or weekly basis to support your personal presence brand by filling in the rest of Figure 2-1.

Stories of Contrasting Actions and Personal Presence Brands

I've had a client named Greg Stock for close to 15 years, since I started my PR firm. When I first met Greg he was the VP of marketing at a technology company that later went public. Today he's the CEO of Vovici, a company that develops enterprisewide online feedback tools such as surveys and analytics to use in building better customer and employee relationships. One of the attributes I've always admired about Greg is that he's masterful at intentionally using his own actions to set a culture and focus attention. He's got a great amount of energy, and if you don't know him, you may just

My personal presence brand values (What do I want to be known for?)	Actions I must take on a regular basis to support this value	Actions I must avoid so I don't undermine this value
Value #1 Example: Accountability	1. Get a firm agreement with clients up-front, so expectations are shared. 2. Listen to the client's concerns fully, and proactively accept what I could have done better. Acknowledge the client's feelings. 3. End with firm solutions going forward that are explicit and in writing. 4. Honor commitments and exceed them early on, to show I got the message.	1. Not taking time to process client issues, so I can put myself in their shoes. 2. Expressing defensiveness in conversation. 3. Promising things I can't deliver. 4. Taking on projects where the client's expectations are unrealistic.
Value #2		
Value #3		

Figure 2-1. Actions to support your personal presence brand.

figure he's someone who has more hours in the day than the rest of us. But in fact, he manages his time well, using it to build his personal presence brand as well as his company's brand.

Greg's background story is very telling: During college, as the drum major in the Penn State Blue Band, Greg had to attempt a full frontal flip before the start of each football game in front of 109,000 screaming fans (and millions of television viewers). Sounds stressful enough, right? But add to that the Penn State tradition: When the drum major makes the flip, Penn State will win the game; when he misses, Penn State will lose. Oh, and by the way, the drum major performs in full uniform, including a 20-inch hat.

So Greg must have been a gymnast, right? Guess again. Greg tried out for the drum major position as a freshman. That was when he did a flip for the first time in his life. He came in second place and went on with student life, not thinking much about it. Then nine days before a game against Temple, Greg got a call that the drum major had fallen during a flip and broken his neck and both wrists. Greg was asked to step in.

Over four days Greg trained for the flip. He was exhausted, sore, and gut-wrenchingly nervous about the game. Let's not forget that the last drum major *broke his neck*. Greg wasn't even able to practice in uniform because of the hasty alterations that had to be made. Finally, it was game day. The fans were screaming. Greg started running and stuck the flip perfectly. He made every flip that year and Penn State won the national championship. Greg was the longest-serving drum major in Penn State history—a five-year streak—and he missed his landing only four times. (Penn State lost each of those four games.) They played in three national championships—the Sugar Bowl, Orange Bowl, and Fiesta Bowl—winning two of them. Today, Greg's legendary flips can be seen on YouTube.

This story tells you quite a bit about Greg's ability to focus his actions behind a goal. Now fast-forward to 2009, when Greg took over as CEO of Vovici. He immediately wanted to focus the company on getting closer to its customers because they held the secret to success, as well as to continual product improvement and market intelligence. Plus, as a provider of software-based products and services for building customer relations, Vovici had an extra incentive.

As Greg explained, "We were in the business of helping companies get closer to their own customers, so if we didn't lead the way, shame on us. We had to be the role models."

The role modeling began with Greg himself. On one of his first days as the new CEO, he showed up unannounced at a routine product-training meeting for customers. He said hello and answered questions about the company. No big agenda. But the fact that he'd made it a point to be there as one of his first orders of business sent a powerful message that customers were a priority. He embarked on a customer road show, meeting face-to-face with a target list of Vovici's top 100 customers. He initiated a customer conference, and then a customer advisory council. He linked every employee's quarterly bonus to customer satisfaction performance goals. And the list goes on.

When you ask Greg how he organizes his time, he'll tell you that when a customer or prospect needs to see him, he's there. No excuses. In fact, when he led an effort to establish new corporate values, No. 1 was "Customers Rule."

With the actions to back up the words coming directly from the top, you can guess how Vovici's employees relate to their customers, and what effect that's had on the company. Since Greg came on board, Vovici has doubled its average deal size and boasts a customer retention rate of 93 percent. In July 2011, the market noticed too, as Vovici was acquired by Verint Systems for $76 million.

Compare that story to Brian, who was also the new CEO of a midsize company. Brian was a whip smart, successful guy who wanted to build a more collaborative company. He inherited a culture that could best be described as adrift, disjointed, and skeptical. In the absence of strong leadership there was a power vacuum from which individual fiefdoms had emerged. The last CEO had ruled with brute force and left heavy emotional carnage in his wake. People were territorial and protective.

Brian came in and saw that there was considerable talent in the company, but scarce collaboration. He gathered all the employees together for a staff meeting and announced that collaboration would be a core value of the group from this day forward. He knew that to role-model collaboration, he needed to be seen as someone who was in the trenches with his people. As Brian stood in front of his group, he meant every word that he said. His intentions were positive and pure.

In the daily chaos of work, however, things got tricky. Brian's core nature was to be an introvert. As a former engineer, he loved to solve problems in his head. His analytical mind worked on hyperspeed; few people could match his intellect. Whenever there was a chance to collaborate with his colleagues to solve a vexing problem, Brian would default to solving it himself and presenting the answer. His team caught on pretty quickly that you shouldn't waste too much time solving a problem when the boss is going to do it his way anyway. Brian's heart was in the right place, but his actions simply didn't support his intention. And his inspired speech about collaboration? Background noise.

We worked to find Brian new actions that supported collaboration. When issues arose, one approach was to hold short sessions immediately where Brian only asked questions to elaborate on the situation—withholding any and all answers. Then he let his team collaborate on solutions. His role was as a coach, not an omniscient guru. It was a difficult change for him, and a constant struggle to combat his own default action. There were times he wanted to scream, "Can't you see the obvious right answer?" But awareness is the first step in change, and he moved perceptions over time. Brian gradually saw that while his employees may approach a problem from another direction, or even at a slower pace than he did, in the end the reward of an engaged team produced longer-term results and enhanced buy-in. He had a clear idea of what actions he should take—and avoid—to support his intention.

Intentional Acting Starts by Paying Attention

Actions are the communications we trust the most. Your work on presence won't get off the ground unless you can begin to notice, and then to understand, and finally to change your micro- and macro-actions.

Right about now you may be thinking, "This is a lot to try and be intentional about. I have to set intentions about my presence in general, and then be intentional about my body language and my actions." Remember one of the promises of this book: You don't have to do everything. Pick and choose what works for you, and what gives you results. There are a lot of ways to improve your presence. Some of them will give you more leverage than others. It's your call.

Key Takeaways from Chapter 2

1. Humans trust actions over all other forms of communications. Actions either underline or undermine your presence.
2. For clarity in your communications, you must have alignment between your intention and your actions, both through micro-actions, such as body language, and macro-actions, such as how you spend your time.
3. You already know how to have perfectly aligned body language in situations where you feel comfortable.
4. Your body naturally knows when it's out of alignment with your intentions. You can monitor your own body language when you give yourself the opportunity to self-observe.
5. Most people need to smile more, especially at work. It improves your presence to others and reinforces good thoughts for yourself.
6. Your actions are like a red blinking light that signals to others "This is important to me."

Ideas I Want to Try from Chapter 2:

_____

_____

_____

_____

_____

_____

CHAPTER 3

Stopping the Negativity Loop

You now know how to think about your presence as a result of creating and living your intentions. All well and good. But what happens when things don't go as intended? Nervousness, anxiety, and insecurity have a way of derailing our most ardent plans—especially when we care greatly about the outcome.

I mentioned in the last chapter that I'm a speaker for Vistage International, which, with 14,000 members, bills itself as the world's leading professional development organization for CEOs. It's a phenomenal organization, and before I became a speaker I was a member for four years. The group has both a high-caliber speakers' list— from which I learned enormously through the years—and smart, experienced members and group chairs. (Susan Scott of *Fierce Conversations* fame ran a Vistage group.)

When I sold my PR firm and started working as a leadership coach, I decided to try to get on the Vistage speakers' circuit. I'd been warned: Becoming a Vistage speaker wouldn't be easy. First, you have to present to a group that scores you. If you score high enough, you live to speak to another group. Maintain a high score, and you stay on the circuit. Vistage members see a new speaker each month, so the material has to be fresh and relevant. Each three-hour workshop must be engaging and informative. Finally, after each talk, it's a Vistage custom for the members go around the table and tell you to your face how they think you did. These are seasoned CEOs in an atmosphere that honors telling it straight. They don't hold back.

In 2008, after weeks of preparation, I led my first Vistage workshop. My talk was on leadership presence. If I didn't present a strong presence myself, I was toast. I've presented with some very high stakes over the years (such as when I was under pressure to make payroll). But this time I was more nervous than ever. I managed to get through it by using many of the concepts in this book. It wasn't my best presentation, but it was my first time, and I got a passing score. I achieved my goal.

Nervousness, anxiety, and insecurity can derail our most ardent plans—especially when we care the most about the outcome.

Then came the second Vistage workshop about a month later. This one was a whole different story. From moment one, I had a hard time connecting with the group. The points that had landed so well before didn't resonate. I use a lot of humor to engage, but unfortunately, this time my jokes fell flat. When a couple of the group members pushed back on some of my points, I let it get argumentative. Instead of listening and handling it with grace, I was completely knocked off balance. Somehow I managed to get through it. The feedback at the end was tough. I felt some of the members questioned my right to be there at all. My scores were average. Not good enough.

But that's just part of the story—the part you can see from the outside. Inside my head was a whirling, spiraling negativity loop. It started even before I uttered one word at the first workshop. I began this endeavor by questioning whether I was good enough to join this exclusive group. I still held some lingering feelings of inadequacy from a childhood fear of public speaking. (Don't laugh: I bombed in front of my entire elementary school in a student council election.) I also questioned how I'd be taken as a then-30-something woman presenting to a group of seasoned executives, many of whom were men. I was not coming from a point of strength and positivity.

After the second presentation, all those negative feelings seemed entirely validated. And I upped the negative ante quite a bit with even more self-defeating thoughts: I didn't know what I was talking about. I wasn't funny or interesting. I'm just not likable enough. I'm going to trash my entire new coaching career. Maybe I should try another profession.

I could go on, but do you see what's happening here? It's a big, fat negativity loop. And when it gets steam, it screams.

So what happened next? I spent days poring over the feedback, ruminating and consoling myself with a few glasses of wine, and then decided to learn from the experience and try harder. I consulted some colleagues for outside advice. I went back to the basics and audited myself against my own presence tactics. I focused on what I could control at that point in time, reworking examples and practicing the content repeatedly, on tape, until my presentation felt natural. The next time I presented to the group, my scores improved and continued to stay high. I even had a few perfect scores later on!

While overcoming obstacles makes a good story, that's not why I bring up this experience. The point is how quickly I spun into the negative and forgot everything I knew about presence. And the more negative I let myself get, the more off balance I was thrown.

Funny enough, when I spoke later with people who were in the workshop that I deemed a disaster, they had a slightly different take. One said my presentation was pretty good for having been only my second one. Another said he learned a lot and has used my material. Someone else told me that that particular group tends to be especially harsh on speakers. Months later, two separate group members even approached me about coaching at their companies.

How could our reactions to the same situation have been so dissimilar? And what happened to get me so negative so fast?

Negative thoughts happen to all of us. You can learn to inoculate yourself and recover faster when destructive, anxious thinking occurs.

I watch clients fall into this same negativity trap all the time. I'm going to guess it's familiar to many of you reading this book. Negative loops destroy intention. They are akin to a heavyweight pro fighting a lightweight amateur. You can win only if you take away the big guy's strength. Luckily, there are ways to inoculate yourself against this kind of destructive, anxious thinking—and to recover faster when it happens.

What Depressed Adolescents Have to Do with Your Presence

About 10 years ago, a field of psychology branded "positive psychology" began getting mainstream attention. Led in part by Martin Seligman, author of *Learned Optimism* and *Authentic Happiness* and also a renowned psychology professor at the University of Pennsylvania, it's permeated many fields including leadership development.[1]

As Seligman explains it, he found his way to positive psychology by virtue of practices he didn't support.[2] Psychology, as he saw it, was mostly about diagnosing and correcting what's wrong. In addition to relying on extensive therapy sessions to analyze the core issue, psychologists were prescribing pharmaceuticals with increasing frequency. Seligman was particularly concerned about the rise in depression diagnoses in preteens and teenagers, which had gone up 10-fold since the 1950s (and continue to increase). Fourteen percent of people between the ages of 12 and 17 experience a major depressive episode.[3] Seligman began to study ways to build resilience into school-age children so that they never experience depression in the first place. After 30 years of hands-on longitudinal research, he discovered that resilience, in fact, could be taught using techniques that we now know as positive psychology.

One of the overarching messages of this research is that by focusing attention on what's right rather than what's wrong, and learning how to be resilient against negativity, we can guard ourselves against protracted setbacks and live a happier, more fulfilling life. Seligman also spawned the idea that we all have signature strengths, and that we are more fulfilled when we are able to apply them in our regular lives. The strengths concept was made even more famous by the Clifton StrengthsFinder, which is an assessment administered by the Gallup Organization and featured in the bestselling book *Now, Discover Your Strengths*.[4]

> Positive psychology shows that resilience can be learned.

Here's why these findings are key to your presence. What positive psychologists are discussing occurs in all aspects of your life. It is deeply embedded in your presence and how you approach the world. Those same pessimistic thoughts are also situational; they become loudest when we are in high-stress situations—*exactly the same kinds of situations when we need our presence to carry us through*.

When we get in situations where we are uncomfortable and our negative thoughts take over, we create a downward spiral. Most of know exactly what this feels like. On the other hand, positivity creates an upward and outward spiral—and resilience to shorten our recovery time. We may still have catastrophic thoughts, but if we recognize them in real time, we can get ourselves back on track—and back to our intention— faster.

> Positivity creates an upward and outward spiral.

Argue Against Your Negativity—and Win!

So how do you cultivate resilience around your presence? Sounds sort of idealistic, I realize. But Seligman offers some practical ways to manage our thought patterns.

Seligman states that pessimistic thoughts have two characteristics: They are permanent and universal. Permanence is the feeling that something is here to stay and won't change. I hear these types of permanent statements from clients frequently: "I'm never good in board meetings" or "He's just difficult to work with." Universal is the idea that the situation is pervasive. Frequent universal statements might be, "I'm not a people person" or "This entire company is unmotivated." As you can see, after my second fateful Vistage presentation, nearly all my thoughts fell into these two categories.

> Pessimistic thoughts are permanent and universal. Optimistic thoughts are temporary and specific.

People who maintain optimistic thoughts gain resilience. When they have setbacks, they see the issue as temporary and specific, not permanent and pervasive. If I had looked at my Vistage talk from an optimistic standpoint, I would have attributed my less-than-stellar performance to situational nervousness (temporary) and to the personalities in this particular group (specific).

And the truth is, I would have done a better job in the first place since I wouldn't have been led off track by the downward spiral.

Seligman argues that you can learn how to dispute your own

negativity and turn it into optimism. I've seen clients learn and apply optimism repeatedly in my work. First you need to recognize those stressed-out thoughts for what they are: catastrophizing with little or no root in reality. Just imagine that a friend came to you with those same negative thoughts. You would easily dispute them.

Friend: I'm never good in meetings. People here don't respect my contribution.

You: Are you kidding? Remember that product brainstorm last month? You had the best ideas on the team. The culture here is to talk all over one another. They do it to everyone.

Friend: I'm bad at motivating other people.

You: Just because you're not a rah-rah kind of manager doesn't mean you're not motivating. You've been very motivating to me. You just do it in a quieter way. I come to you for advice because you're thoughtful and honest. Your team sees the same qualities in you. You simply need to work on pumping up the team more in meetings.

Your work is to get really good at turning pessimism into optimism as soon as it surfaces, even if it's in the moment. Having actual labels to apply to this thinking deflates it. Is it permanent and universal? I am frequently in conversation with clients who know exactly what they want to say and how they want to say it, but who worry about how they'll manage setbacks in the moment. They are anxious that their nervousness will overtake their competency if *everything* doesn't go *right*. And life rarely does. You can derail quickly if you play the "what if" game.

How often have you found yourself in a similar situation? How about when the stakes are high, outcomes matter, and you want to maintain your composure? Most important, you want to stay in alignment between your intention and your communications. Is it easy for you to stay on task when things go awry? Or do you find yourself getting tripped up and distracted?

You can practice turning your thoughts around to stay on track, whether in the middle of a stressful situation or in day-to-day encounters. I've populated Figure 3-1 with a few examples that come

Pessimistic Thoughts (Permanent and Universal)	Optimistic Thoughts (Temporary and Specific)
I'm too busy at work to focus on my own leadership abilities.	This quarter has been a particularly busy time in my job. If I can't make time soon for professional development, then I'll need to make some changes.
My boss never recognizes my achievements.	Lately my boss has been distracted and hasn't seen my work product.
I don't have what it takes to get promoted here.	Communications skills are valued here, so I'll work to augment mine or find a position that rewards my abilities.
I always get nervous in front of groups and I don't come across well.	I sometimes get nervous when I first begin speaking to unfamiliar groups.

[Enter your thoughts here]

_____

_____

_____

_____

_____

_____

Figure 3-1. Turning pessimistic thoughts into optimism.

up in my work with executives. See if you can fill in some of your own thoughts and turn your pessimism into optimism.

When you arrange the statements side-by-side, it becomes apparent that these pessimistic thoughts, whether spoken or held, are invalid and all-around unhelpful. They support inaction, excuse complacency, and take away our options for solutions. They destroy our game.

Pessimism spreads insidiously in ourselves and in our companies. Now you have a tool to fight back. Listen for pessimism lurking and make an effort to refute it, in any or all of these three ways:

1. Notice and negate your own pessimistic thoughts and words. This step alone will change your orientation as well as how others orient around you.
2. Look around you for pessimism in real time, as it occurs—in strategy meetings, delegation situations, or performance reviews. When pessimism is rearing its ugly head, don't mindlessly buy into it. Instead, call it what it is.
3. Be a force for optimism. You can be a beacon for resilience and help others to recognize how their negative thinking is holding them (and those around them) back. Your presence will only benefit.

Game On: Get Yourself in the Zone

Many of you may be reading this book specifically because you want to work on your presence in high-pressure situations, whether it's a job interview or a presentation to your board of directors. That's often when we rely on our presence the most. It's important to be resilient when you get anxious or thrown off track, but even better if you can prevent yourself from getting there in the first place.

I am a huge believer in cultivating a repeatable process for getting yourself into the zone. Executives can practice these "pregame rituals" just like athletes do before they take the field. They don't have to be elaborate. The ritual may be listening to a favorite song, taking a moment to pause and visualize success, or even joking with a friend. It's unique to the person

A pregame ritual is a repeatable process for getting yourself in the zone of your intention.

and relevant to that person's intention. Pregame rituals dispel nerves and put you in a positive frame of mind to succeed. An effective ritual also gives you confidence that if it worked once it will work again.

Pregame Rituals That Work

One of my coaching clients, Jan, was a partner in a global law firm. In the midst of a critical case, she was heading up a large legal team of associates and other partners. Jan was in charge of client relations. Unfortunately, her client contact was proving to be a difficult personality for her. Jan found this person intimidating, aggressive, and mistrustful of the firm. Several times a week there were large group conference calls with the client where everyone came away feeling beaten up and beleaguered. During our coaching sessions, Jan asked how she could psych herself up to manage these calls more effectively. She wanted to maintain her ground for her team, and also to build a more trustful relationship with the client. Jan wisely knew that if she felt defensive and demotivated during these conference calls, her team would follow suit and performance could suffer. She also realized that simply anticipating the calls made her anxious. She was in a negative spiral.

We started trying out various pregame rituals to get Jan in the frame of mind for her stated intention: staying grounded and open. She wanted to be positive and feel confident in her team's work, and to be able to push back when it was warranted, without coming across as defensive. We tried various approaches, such as preparing talking points to focus on, practicing deep breathing, using imagery, and even rallying with other team members in advance of the call. Finally, what worked best for her was to shut her office door for five minutes before each call and focus on a photo of her kids. It gave her a sense of joy, took her mind off the negative, and reminded her of what was really important. It was simple. And more important, it worked.

Here's a different scenario; in fact, it's my own pregame ritual. When I had my PR firm, we were constantly going on new business pitches—essentially "bake-offs" where three or more firms would come in, one after the other, and sell their best ideas to the potential client. I knew that our ideas alone would not win us the business. At that point in the vetting process, all the firms at the table had good ideas. We would get picked if we exhibited the most creativity and energy, because that's what makes a PR team successful. I wanted our presence to show precisely those two traits. Frequently, I would take staff members on these pitches. Some of them were neither comfortable nor experienced meeting face-to-face with powerful executives sitting across from them at a large conference table. I needed a pregame ritual to allay their nerves and get all of us "in the zone" together. My ritual was that from the minute we piled into the car until after the sales meeting, we did not talk about the presentation. We weren't cramming final thoughts into our PowerPoint presentation or rehearsing nuanced points. That would create more stress around the wrong thing. I made sure our discussion was purely fun. We made jokes, talked about weekend plans, gossiped, or played loud music.

What a great first impression we made! The potential client saw a group of smiling, excited people who genuinely enjoyed working together. I believe that pregame ritual was responsible for our amazing 90 percent win rate from final-round meetings. Or, to put it another way, I know for certain that our success wasn't because of bullet 2 on PowerPoint slide 12.

Develop Your Own Pregame Ritual

To develop your own stress-mitigating pregame ritual, start by asking yourself these questions:

- What usually puts me in a good mood?
- When am I most relaxed?

Your answers will give you some clues about what makes you feel centered and authentic. Then try out some of these ideas right before your next event:

- Listen to a favorite song that pumps you up (Tom Petty's "I Won't Back Down" does it for me every time) or calms you down (perhaps a classical, jazz, or new age selection).
- Spend five minutes of quiet time alone, eyes closed, focusing on your intention. Try to sit in an open position with your feet flat on the floor and your arms resting on your thighs.
- Look at a meaningful object such as a photo, vacation souvenir, award, or gift that reminds you of a time when you were at your best.

- Think of a time when you have been shown sincere gratitude. Relive as much of the detail from the experience as possible, including how you felt in that moment.
- Visualize the entire experience going well. See yourself succeeding at the things you feel most anxious about.
- Call a good friend or colleague and have a few laughs. If you are at the event or meeting, seek out people who are friendly and exchange a funny story or joke.
- Select clothes that you feel great in. (This piece of advice may sound shallow, but for a lot of people, putting on a power suit or a lucky tie helps.)

|||||||||||||||||||||||||||||||||||||||||||||||||||||||||||||||||||||||||||||||||||||||||||||||||||||||||||||||||||||||||||||||||

In the Moment: Can Sweaty Palms Be Merely Interesting?

For many of us, understanding the negative spiral and having a great pregame ritual still won't completely alleviate a physical reaction to a stress situation in the moment. And often it's the physical reactions that trip us up more than anything. Heart pounding, hands shaking, sweating, losing our thoughts—hardly anyone has escaped the symptoms.

When your physical reactions take over, it's easy to forget your intention and lose your bearings. Before you know it, you're in a negative downward spiral and thinking, "I'm going to mess up. This is going horribly. Everyone can see I'm nervous. Just get this over with. . . ." But a case of nerves doesn't have to turn into a potential presence buster. Here are reliable strategies to get back to your presence objective when communicating in any type of group situation.

Often it's the physical reactions to stress that trip us up more than anything.

Take deep breaths. This is the oldest trick in the book, but it stays there because it works! Often nerves begin to escalate right before you start speaking. When that happens, take a few deep breaths—four counts in, four counts out. The deeper the better.

Start from a position of strength. Nervousness thrives in insecurity. Start your discussion or presentation with comfortable material. If you have a limited time to rehearse, make sure you go through the beginning multiple times. If you do well and get a good response in the first few minutes, often your nervousness will subside.

Pause. Pauses are natural in a conversation. They allow both speaker and listener to collect their thoughts, and they provide transitions between topics. They are not to be feared or avoided. When we get nervous, we tend to talk quickly and avoid pauses. It's perfectly fine to take a second to regain your composure if you forget a point. Don't let it derail you. In general, it's not the pause we notice as much as the speaker's reaction to her own pause. I've seen magnetic presenters make prolonged pauses look entirely deliberate. I've also watched people laugh at their own forgetfulness and just go on to the next point. (I once saw a comedian lose his train of thought for several seconds in a live monologue and then create a 10-minute gag out of it.) The audience is more forgiving than you think.

Create a dialogue. Often what creates anxiety is the fact that, as the discussion leader or presenter, the entire event rests on your shoulders. You are busy trying to remember exactly what to say and how to say it. Try taking some of the pressure off by creating a conversation early on where you elicit response by playing the role of facilitator. This works for any size group. Ask a large group a question and tease out answers. Start a small, one-on-one meeting by asking the other person what he wants to get out of the conversation. It takes the focus off of you and allows for a more relaxed interaction. It can also set up your points by creating shared examples you can refer back to later.

Practice acknowledging and isolating the physical reaction. A good friend who is an actor once told me, "Don't fight with your nerves. You'll lose." Later, when I read *Leadership Presence* by Belle Linda Halpern and Kathy Lubar,[5] I loved how they applied the same advice. Halpern and Lubar are cofounders of The Ariel Group, a consulting firm of trained performance artists who use dramatic techniques to help leaders improve their effectiveness. They describe it as "Let thoughts go, let feelings be." The idea is that even performers at the top of their craft get nervous. It's a physical reaction. Instead of fighting it and resisting, learn to observe it and acknowledge it as purely a physical effect with no link to your ability to perform effectively. When your heart starts racing, simply think, "That's interesting" or "It's really pounding now." Accept the feeling. Dwell on it for a moment. Perhaps even name it: "There's my crazy telltale heart again." But don't conclude that it will make you unsuccessful. Often when the anxiety kicks in, the act of resisting creates a negative spiral because we usually can't stop our reaction. It creates fear. This technique isolates it, acknowledges it, and enables us to move on.

If It Doesn't Come Easy, Join the Club

If this chapter hits home, you're in good company. You can have a penchant for pessimistic thoughts and nerves galore and still have excellent presence. Most successful executives I know have struggled with these challenges and learned to overcome them, even if they never go away entirely. Your presence gets better when you understand what's happening and develop some coping mechanisms. It also helps to remember that we notice far more about our own mistakes than anyone else does. At times, the best thing we can do is to give ourselves a break.

Key Takeaways from Chapter 3

1. Nearly everyone struggles with nervousness, anxiety, and insecurity in high-pressure situations where we care deeply about the outcome. It happens to even the most successful and dynamic communicators.
2. It's easy to find yourself caught in a downward negative spiral with your thoughts, feelings, and actions following suit. Stay vigilant and recognize when it's purely pessimism and not constructive.

3. Pessimistic thoughts are permanent and universal. Optimistic thoughts are temporary and specific. Learn to challenge your thoughts before, during, and after a stressful situation.
4. A pregame ritual—a repeatable process to get yourself in the zone of your intention—can be a powerful way to get into a positive frame of mind from the outset.
5. When you have a physical reaction in a stressful situation, accept that it's a normal response and use helpful strategies to work around it. Trying to tamp down the reaction or resist it usually makes it worse.

Ideas I Want to Try from Chapter 3:

_____

_____

_____

_____

_____

CHAPTER 4

Presence as Perception

Even though professionals are extolled to exhibit an executive presence, when you push for what that means you'll find a variety of answers. Maybe you've had that experience yourself trying to get to the bottom of your own feedback. So while there's buzz, there's also confusion.

Earlier in this book, I posited several reasons why I believe there's such an emphasis on presence. Perhaps it's due to the evolving structure of decentralized companies or a sign of generational shifts in leadership. Whatever the cause, the effect is certain. People are being asked to strengthen the way they communicate and connect with others to increase their influence in looser and more disparate corporate structures.

It's natural to describe executive presence in terms of first impressions or public-speaking skills. Those are definable, trainable concepts to grasp. But think more broadly about your presence. After all, presence exists in more than one area of our lives. Sure, we may be more proficient at certain aspects of our communications than others, but the concepts of presence in this book are far-reaching and vastly applicable.

Presence is the way we move through the world.

When I went through Georgetown University's Leadership Coaching program to be accredited as a coach, part of the training was about noticing how people *move through the world*. To me, that expresses the essence of presence. It is the most basic form of communications that we possess.

When you think about presence in those terms, you realize the effect that building a stronger one can have, not just on your job but on your life as well. For example, if you are reading this book because you want to be more self-assured in the face of difficult conversations, you may start to look outside the conference room. Your intention to be more proactive about having conversations with other people could create a whole new dynamic for your life. And as you grow more confident in your ability to tackle tough issues with grace, that newfound skill can spur you to consider other areas of your presence that could use some work.

The expansiveness of presence can be overwhelming. As if it's not hard enough to deal with your boss adding "executive presence" to your developmental goals, now I'm asking you to think of presence as being an outward expression of you as a person. Even more challenging: There's not one right way to show your presence. It's an amorphous concept, yet it has power over the jobs we get, how much we earn, and the quality of our relationships. But remember that we are all presence observers. We see it immediately in other people—and it can be enormously helpful to tap into that expertise for a better understanding of ourselves.

> *Presence is an amorphous concept with defined power over our lives.*

This chapter covers how to get a baseline read on your own presence so that you can determine how others experience you and what behaviors are getting in the way of your intention. For some of you, this process is going to be daunting. Asking our friends, colleagues, and family what they truly think of us feels embarrassing, private, and self-absorbed. It requires you to face some aspects of yourself you might not like so much. It could leave you open to a personal affront.

I'm going to ask you to put those feelings aside for now. Because if you pursue the answers with an open mind and a brave heart, the knowledge you receive about your presence is life changing. Seeing yourself as others do is not only a rare gift, it's transformative.

Is Your Presence a Reflection of You or Me?

You may be saying, "Hold on. Isn't this book supposed to be about authenticity? Why does it matter so much what other people think?"

Here's the deal with presence: It's part communicating in alignment with your intention and part being *received* with clarity. You can't figure out how you are doing on the latter without some sort of feedback, formal or otherwise. Finding out the effect you have on others gives you a helpful framework for focusing on your own presence.

Getting feedback is necessary. Pursue it, digest it, and internalize it. Most important, keep in your mind the entire time that there's no right way to have a strong presence. One size does not fit all. Much of how we experience others is filtered through our own experiences and completely biased. One person may gravitate toward the strong way you open a meeting, while you will seem overly brash to someone else because you remind him of a dictatorial former coworker. You are viewed through others' subjectivity. It reminds me of a great piece of wisdom: When someone says something unkind to you, it's more about that person than it is about you. You can't see that when you're a teenager, but it gets easier with life experience (even if it still packs a punch).

Any feedback you give or receive is subjective. But it's still valuable. Your job as you go about gathering feedback is to seek the common themes that keep appearing, which will help you understand how others see you.

It is a delicate balance to understand other people's perspectives, communicate so that they are best able to hear what you are saying, and remain true to yourself. People with great presence do it very well. Part 2 provides useful strategies for conceptualizing and achieving this balancing act.

Before we get to that though, you'll do yourself a big favor if you begin to understand how you are perceived in general terms. What you find may surprise you or confirm what you already know. Regardless, it's guaranteed to be interesting.

How to Get Your Personal Presence Audit in an Hour or Less

The process of collecting feedback from other people is remarkably easy. I do it every day for my clients. Usually, after asking a few short questions, I'll hear everything I need to know. With the right questions, the themes emerge and repeat themselves throughout the interview. In less than an hour, I have the data for an entire year's worth of a person's executive development.

Initiating and internalizing the feedback *for yourself* is, by comparison, remarkably difficult. For all the reasons I just mentioned, it can be uncomfortable to ask people you trust what they really think of you. Then, after you get the feedback, it's impossible to keep your own ego out of the process. It feels great to hear the positive. Bring it on! (Even if we publicly shy away from the accolades, in the privacy of our own mind it's incredibly affirming.) But the negative makes us feel as if we have to explain ourselves. Not only do we fear that part of feedback, but we tend to let it marinate for days on end. The positive, meanwhile, is quickly forgotten.

This process won't be time-intensive. In fact, you'll be shocked at how little time it takes. However, it may be psychically intensive for you. You may be tempted to avoid it altogether. Or you promise to do it but keep putting it off. You may be flipping to the next chapter right now. If so, stop!

Realize that this is not a comfortable activity for most people. Then do it anyway. The small amount of time reaps big rewards. It's the most powerful exercise in this entire book.

||||||||||||||||||||||||||||||||||||||||||||||||||||||||||||||||||||||||||||||||||||||||||||||||||||||||

Corporate 360s vs. a Presence Audit

When I begin a coaching relationship with an executive, I typically do two things: (1) read any existing reviews or development plans and (2) conduct my own feedback process. Often the corporate review includes a 360-degree instrument where colleagues, supervisors, and direct reports have offered anonymous feedback, which the review preparer has factored into the final conclusions.

If you have participated in these corporate-sponsored, often electronically administered 360-degree reviews, then you know the inherent issues with them. First, people rarely give honest feedback knowing that a colleague's future is at stake. If they like their coworkers, they don't want to hurt their career. If they don't like them, their feedback can be vitriolic and personal. Often people fear retribution. Anonymity is always suspect. While I wouldn't call it a waste of time because you can always learn something, the utility of the standard 360-degree review is limited.

If you have this type of 360-degree feedback from your workplace, it won't be enough, by itself, to give you a personal presence audit. It's not sufficient in my work for clients, and it's not the full picture for you. The reason I review these documents is to help me formulate the right questions to ask going forward. These existing reviews also give me a sense of what my clients have heard so far from other people, and what, if anything, they have done about it. Most important for this conversation, if executive presence is an issue but has not been overtly mentioned, I can usually find it described as a euphemism or a catchall phrase somewhere in the feedback. Unlike hard and definable functional skills, presence issues can be lumped into broad categories. Here are some common phrases I've seen written on reviews that allude to presence issues.

You May Have a Presence Problem if Your Reviews Say . . .

- Lacks strong communications skills
- Doesn't command respect
- Not motivating to others
- Needs to be more seasoned
- Doesn't run meetings well
- Not leadership material
- Has trouble carrying a room
- Not someone others identify with
- Behind-the-scenes person/not client-facing

Increasingly, people are told that they could use some help with executive presence without getting a meaningful description of what executive presence actually is. These reviews help uncover the presenting issues.

Conduct Your Presence Audit

As part of my feedback process for clients, I conduct my own assessment. You might not be fortunate enough to have an executive coach to collect this feedback for you—and you don't need one if you follow the straightforward, four-step process I outline here. This is where I get to the presence questions and uncover the essence of how a person is perceived. In other words, it's where the juice is. You don't need 15 people to get actionable, meaty feedback. For the purposes of this exercise, you need only five. But you need the right five.

Step 1: Pick the Right People

Select five people you know and trust to be part of your feedback circle. Choose people who are accustomed to seeing you in the kinds of situations where you are looking for feedback. If they know you in more than one aspect of your life (e.g., a work colleague who also plays on your softball team; a board member you socialize with occasionally; a boss you've worked for more than once), it's even better. While it is important that you trust the people and find them credible, make sure you don't just choose people that you like. You want to ask for feedback from people who will give you their unedited opinion. Steer clear of those who avoid conflict or tend to soft-pedal. Don't simply ask friends because it seems easier (unless of course they fit the criteria). You want the feedback to count. So keep in mind that sometimes the best observations come from people we've held at arm's length.

Step 2: Ask for Participation

Without question, this is the hardest part, so you have to frame your request correctly. You want the people in your feedback circle to know that you are sincere, that you won't hold a grudge, and that you are seeking feedback for your own personal development. Explain that it's not about what any one person says, but what themes emerge from the group. This can help ease the burden for the people participating and allow them to speak more freely.

Here are two examples of how you might approach others about their participation:

> *Tom, I've always appreciated your candor in tough situations at work. You speak your mind, which I respect. I want to ask you a personal favor. I'm trying to get a handle on how I'm really*

perceived at work. It's difficult to get straight feedback, and I need it to get to the next level. It would mean a lot to me if you would be willing to offer your perspective. I'm talking to a few people, so your feedback would be part of a bigger process. You have my word that it will only be between the two of us and it won't impact our relationship. Would you be willing to share your thoughts?

Or:

Joan, may I ask a favor of you? I've gotten review feedback and it's not as direct as I'd like. I'm asking a few close friends whose opinion I trust to give their candid thoughts on how I'm viewed at work. I'd really appreciate your input. Of course, I understand this is just your informal opinion and would stay between the two of us.

These conversations are most effective face-to-face. If that doesn't work, the telephone is the next best option. (Email is notoriously bad for communicating nuanced messages. It also doesn't allow you to clarify any points you don't understand. It invites misinterpretation.)

The rest is up to you. You can choose to collect feedback casually, say, over coffee or a beer. Or you can make a formal appointment and have the discussion over a desk. Pick the venue that fits your style and comfort level.

Step 3: Ask Two Simple Yet Powerful Questions
You don't need a complicated set of questions to get good feedback. Presence is the way we move through the world; so ask direct questions that get to the heart of how you are perceived as you move through the world.

1. What's the general perception of me?
2. What could I do differently that would have the greatest impact on my success?

Depending on the person, you'll get answers that range in quality from brilliantly incisive to opaque. You may get overly specific answers because they are safer responses. Often the feedback may be too job-related, such as, "You're great at financial analysis." If that's the case, give one clarifier, such as:

What I mean is, what's the general perception of me as a leader/colleague/person?

It's highly unlikely that someone will mention your presence per se. So, keep in mind the types of catchall phrases that are routinely used to hint at presence problems (as listed earlier in this chapter, in the sidebar "Corporate 360s vs. a Presence Audit").

Step 4: Manage Your Own Reaction

You'll get information that's as good as your ability to receive it. People will be looking to see what effect their feedback has on you *in real time*. Even though you are the one soliciting the feedback, every cell in your body will want to explain and defend yourself. You may be avoiding eye contact, even wincing. If on the phone, you might feel a need to chime in too quickly. So the advice here is simple: Pay attention to your own presence during this feedback process.

Remember all the aspects of presence that we discussed in Chapters 1 and 2. Set an intention for how you want to present yourself during the feedback process. Do a body check to make sure your physical presence is in alignment with your intention. Is your body language open?

Finally, listen. I mean really listen. Don't interrupt. Don't offer explanations or make excuses. If you ask questions, they should be only to clarify: "Can you give me some more description around that?" or "What are some examples of that behavior that you've seen?"

After you receive the feedback, invite your colleague to share any ideas that may come up later. Then smile and express sincere gratitude. Say thank-you for the gift you've just been given.

Post-Feedback: How to Create a Personal Presence Development Plan

After you complete the audit you'll have five people's opinions. I find it's best to write all the feedback down on paper after each interview. Then at the end, go back and look for similarities and themes. If only one person mentions an issue, tuck it away for later. It might be that one person's perspective alone. If several people mention the same strength or weakness, then you're on to something.

From that list, narrow the feedback down to two or three strengths and two or three weaknesses around your presence. The strengths are important. These are the qualities that make you successful. Figure out a way to do more of them.

Your challenges represent where you can grow. Those are the goals you keep top of mind while you are working on your presence. They're your highest leverage points.

Notice that I didn't ask you to address 10 attributes. You don't need to boil the ocean here. You're better off making major strides in a few areas than small changes across many areas.

Presence shortcut: Try to use your strengths to overcome your weaknesses.

You now have your own Personal Presence Development Plan. Here's the best part: You can use your strengths to shore up your weaknesses. As you lay out your strengths and weaknesses together (Figure 4-1 is a sample form you can use), consider where applying more of what you are successful at already doing could fill in your deficits and make a commitment to improve upon them.

I'll provide a quick example. Sometimes I use this exercise as part of a corporate workshop where participants interview each other for feedback. At the end of one such workshop, a big, burly man in his 50s came barreling up to me. He was smiling from ear to ear and had a twinkle in his eye, and he gave me a hearty handshake. He made me laugh with his first comment and I could tell he enjoyed a sense of fun. He exuded it. I wasn't surprised to hear that sense of humor was one of his thematic strengths. He seemed like the type of fellow everyone loved to be around. However, one of his presence challenges was presenting his ideas in a compelling manner.

My overall intention for my presence (or personal presence brand) is:

_____

_____

_____

My top presence strengths:

_____

_____

My commitment to use them daily:

_____

_____

My commitment to use them long term:

_____

_____

_____

My presence challenges:

_____

_____

My commitment to improve upon them daily (using my strengths, if possible):

_____

_____

My commitment to improving upon them long term (again using strengths):

_____

_____

_____

What success looks like:

_____

_____

_____

Figure 4-1.   Personal Presence Development Plan.

In that setting, he explained, he felt he needed to be more serious and to the point. I challenged him to find a way to bring his fun and lively self to situations where he needed to explain concepts to others. At that, his face lit up with an epiphany. He told me a story about how he had bombed a speech in high school by opening with a joke that got booed. So for 40 years he had been under the assumption that he needed to be serious when presenting information to a group. We discussed how his humor served a great purpose— he could use it to put people at ease. Furthermore, he could use his natural storytelling ability to bring complicated concepts to life. In other words, he could use his strengths to overcome a weakness.

Figure out how you can use your strengths. Show the world more of who you are, not less.

One last point about feedback: It can be helpful to enlist one or two trusted colleagues to be an ongoing resource for you. When you decide what you want to focus on, let them know and ask them to be on the lookout for your progress. Give them carte blanche to provide feedback at any time if they see improvement or lack thereof. It can be a major asset to have ongoing feedback as an additional navigation system to keep you on course throughout your life.

Ted Leonsis: What an Indelible, Focused, and Happy Personal Presence Brand Looks Like

In all my experiences observing and working with leaders, Ted Leonsis stands out for having one of the most articulate personal presence intentions I've ever experienced.[1] His approach might not be relevant to everyone, but its lessons are applicable for anyone. Ted is a dynamic and happy person, and his example sums up many of the concepts discussed throughout Part 1 on intentional presence.

What may jump out at you at first about Ted is that he's staggeringly, supernaturally successful. The child of Greek immigrants who grew up in a Brooklyn tenement, he boasts a personal net worth of around $1 billion.

But Ted's model for intentional leadership isn't about being rich; it's about being happy. He lives by a strict principle that the pursuit of a happy and fulfilling life directly creates business success—and he's quick to tell you that it's not the other way around.

Sports fans know Ted as the charismatic owner of the Washington Capitals—a visionary who bought a hockey team with a dwindling fan base and turned it into a top-ranked competitor playing for sold-out crowds. Washingtonians also know Ted as an early supporter (and now owner) of the Verizon Center, a year-round sports and entertainment arena that singlehandedly revitalized an entire washed-out sector of downtown D.C. He also owns the Washington, D.C., men's and women's basketball teams, the Wizards and the Mystics.

But before any of that, Ted was an enterprising technology entrepreneur. He started his first company at age 24, and sold it when he was 26, for $15 million. He sold his second company, Redgate Communications, to AOL for $60 million. He spent the next 13 years there as president and is widely credited as the creative mind that put AOL on the map.

While Ted says he's always had goals, it took a near-fatal plane crash to make him a master at intentionality. When Ted was 28 and living the posh life of a newly minted millionaire, he had a moment of reckoning. As his plane circled the airport preparing for a crash landing, he realized if he died that day, he would die unhappy. He made a bucket list of 101 things he wanted to do, and set about to create a fulfilled life. That list has become legend. Everyone who has worked with him knows about it. To this day, he keeps it posted online with items regularly checked off.

His experiences pursuing his list have produced a clear personal navigation system. Ted makes sure that his presence is about having a positive impact on the lives of others. He calls it the "double bottom line"—financial and humanitarian.

Each year Ted takes the time to talk to an entrepreneurial mentoring group, and I sit on the group's board. Everyone who meets Ted has the same reaction: *That guy has it figured out.* Ted exudes positivity. He's extremely likable, down to earth, humble, and always willing to share with entrepreneurs his secrets to happiness, such as living by goals, building connections through community, and giving back.

Ted walks the walk. He's known for being the most accessible sports team owner ever—even responding to fan emails within 24 hours. He blogs religiously and uses Facebook widely. He gives millions of dollars (and his own time) to charity. (One of the goals on his life list is to donate $100 million.) He's a major supporter of Hoop Dreams, a program that sends disadvantaged kids to college, and he speaks frequently about one young man he personally mentored who has become a surrogate son. A few years ago, he began producing documentary films about neglected social issues, a genre he coined "filmanthropy." (One film, *Nanking*, won an Emmy—another item checked off Ted's list.)

When you meet with Ted, whether you are a sports fan, a young entrepreneur, or a corporate mogul, you feel a little better for it. And that's precisely what Ted intends.

Last Thoughts About Intention and Getting Your Head Around Presence

We started in your head—your thought patterns—because it's where presence begins. Whether actively creating intentions, ensuring that your actions underline those intentions, or containing a negative spiral, you build a stronger presence from the inside out. The chapters in this first part are all about your *intentional* presence, which is the first "I" of I-Presence.

You may decide to settle here for a while before moving forward in the book. You could spend an entire year working on your thought patterns and it wouldn't be wasted—some people dedicate their whole lives to this practice. Or you can use what you learned so far about your potential (and what gets in your way) to push through to Part 2, which explains the second "I" of I-Presence: *individual* connections. Next, we are going to talk about how to forge stronger connections with others and increase your influence and impact on the world around you.

Key Takeaways from Chapter 4

1. Presence is broad and far-reaching. It's the essence of how we move through the world.
2. Authentic presence is a delicate balancing act of understanding other people's perspectives, communicating so that they can best hear you, and staying true to yourself.

3. One of the greatest gifts you can give yourself is to learn how you are truly perceived by others. You can get all the feedback you need in an hour or less if you select the right people to ask.

4. Create your own Personal Presence Development Plan of your strengths and weaknesses. Many of your challenges can be overcome by leveraging your strengths—being more of who you already are, not less.

Ideas I Want to Try from Chapter 4:

_____

_____

_____

_____

_____

PART 2

INDIVIDUAL

Forging Strong Relationships

CHAPTER 5

Go Ahead, Trip Over
Your Own Perfectionism

Up until now the discussion was all about intention—understanding it, creating it, and keeping it. In cultivating executive presence, intention is your aim. It creates the basis from which everything else follows. By practicing intentionality, your presence will benefit immensely, even if you do nothing else. But if you want to build the kind of compelling presence that draws others to you, then you need not just intention, but connection.

The second part of I-Presence is about *individual* connections—how we bring people closer to us, invite them in, and build trust. If intention is your aim, then individual connections are your target. In the workplace, strong connections make us more productive employees, better coworkers, and motivating leaders. Connections provide us with influence, a critical art that has reached must-have status in a marketplace where the old rules don't always apply. Once upon a time, when you wanted to win someone over you'd do it informally; you'd walk down the hall for a friendly chat or catch up at happy hour. But when your colleagues are scattered across the country (or around the world), that becomes considerably harder to pull off. Furthermore, workflow has broken free from the boundaries of strict hierarchies, with many projects getting done through a web of matrices that require relational influence and personal connection.

Connections are tricky: We must wait for an invitation to connect to someone. Access to others is granted, not automatically conferred. Sheer will or endurance doesn't work here (in fact, it usually has the opposite effect). We can spot someone pushing too hard from a mile away.

Access to others is granted, not automatically conferred.

For leaders, and in particular those new to leadership positions, it is a frustrating experience to learn that your title only gets you obedience (if you're lucky). Winning over hearts and minds requires a nuanced approach of making yourself someone others want to trust and follow.

You may already be a natural at building close relationships. You may be someone who easily makes friends, both inside and outside the workplace. Perhaps you work in sales and relationship building is a critical success factor that you've mastered for your job. If that's the case, you may wonder why I've even included a chapter on this topic. It's because for many others, it's not so cut-and-dried. And connections built around work and management are especially tricky. In the course of my work, I often hear people discuss the challenge of making individual connection. For example:

"As the leader, I'm close to some people on my team but can't seem to get through to others."

"I'm not sure how much people buy into my vision."

"I don't know how to play the political game at the office. It's hard to figure out whom to trust."

"I have some good relationships in my immediate work group, but no one else here knows me very well."

"I tolerate my boss/colleague/client, but I don't like her."

"I have a full life outside of work, but I keep it totally separate."

"My client often goes around me to someone more senior."

"I've tried everything to get him to improve his performance, but I can't seem to make a difference."

Rather than present a strict program of must-do practices, I'm going to explore how we make connections authentically and suggest some avenues that should feel natural and right to you. The exercises in this chapter and throughout Part 2 can help you determine if there's "static" in your connections to others so that you can get clearer communications all around. In the process, I hope to also illuminate the ways to build connections at work that propel careers and create more daily joy in the workplace. It just may be the opposite of what you think.

Approachability Creates Hard Business Outcomes

Some of you may already be raising your guard, concerned that we are venturing into touchy-feely territory. To a certain extent you would be right. This isn't a bellicose leadership book about forcing your people into submission. But connection creates powerful business outcomes that you need to do your job well and advance your career. Don't confuse so-called "soft skills" with weakness. People want to work with people they like. If you're someone with whom your colleagues want to work, you're going to have more opportunities thanks to your portable business network that's so essential these days.

Without multiple connection points, you'll be excluded from the critical undercurrent of information that flows through companies. You know what it feels like when you start a new job at a company where you don't yet have trusted sources. When you need information, but you're given only the company line, you're lost. You need the real story, or the subtext of the culture, to be truly effective in your work. Though

> *You need multiple connection points in a company to get the full undercurrent of workplace communications.*

information is more available than ever through instant electronic communications, online communities, and social media, it's also harder than ever to sift through and determine what's valid. Trusted individual connection is the only way to separate rumor from fact. You need information, and you need interpretation.

This need for direct lines of communication becomes even more critical for leaders: They need it the most but find it hardest to come by. In an article in *Harvard Business Review,* Stanford management professor Robert Sutton wrote about the fallacy of centrality—the flawed assumption that because leaders are in the middle of things they have all the information to lead effectively.[1] Sutton cites studies showing that leadership actually makes people more self-absorbed and less attuned to others' perspectives. Add to this "toxic tandem" (Sutton's description) the fact that people searching for information watch every move leaders make, and it can create a ricochet effect of disconnection and disaffection. Leaders need to be vigilant!

One important way to prevent this toxic tandem is to keep reliable information flowing back to the leader about what's happening in the organization, what problems are emerging, and how the leader is perceived. It takes a certain comfort level, and guts, to speak truth to power. This won't happen without a leadership presence that fosters connection and approachability. There are many companies where, to the organizations' detriment, honest feedback to leadership doesn't happen. I had a front-row seat watching dozens of Internet companies implode overnight in the technology bust of 2000 because no one would tell the emperor he had no clothes. But boy, did everyone talk afterward.

Balancing Competency and Vulnerability

Whether you are a leader or not, without connection you will lack presence. You may have perfect oratory skills, deliver impeccable work, and have the focus of a laser, but if you aren't someone that others relate to on a human level, you will at best be admired but never fully trusted.

Connection increases when you balance competency with vulnerability.

Which brings me to what I believe is the core of this relatedness or connection as it relates to presence: a person's ability to balance competency with vulnerability. *Balance* is the operative word here. Too much competency can be intimidating. Too much vulnerability can be read as weakness and ineffectiveness. So, by no means am I saying that you should share your deepest secrets at work, or promote an office culture where group hugs are expected. We're not going there. But when we show our power alongside our humanity, others will connect to us. It's the combination that creates great presence.

This notion of showing vulnerability can be hard for successful executives to digest. I've had a fair share of initial pushback on this point from clients, until they see the effect in practice, either by trying to communicate differently themselves or by observing someone they admire in action. There's cultural pressure at play: Somewhere along the way, in business schools and popular culture, we developed the idea that we must hold back our real selves to be effective at work. It probably started with the tightly wound capitalistic culture of the 1980s, when our role models were Wall Street executives (or actors playing them) who seemed to have it all by being serious, relentless, and unilaterally focused on business success. We're a long way from that time, but I still glimpse vestiges of that culture in the work world. Being called "all business" may not be as much of a compliment as it used to be, but it's not quite an insult, either. While we may take offense at corporations that prioritize profits over people in general terms, corporate extremism across industries has been a recurring story line for three decades.

Consider what qualities make for a great boss or colleague. I've gone through this exercise in multiple settings with various audiences across different industries. The answers are always the same: Most of what makes a leader or colleague memorable to us is the connection piece. "All business" is never how we describe the people who have meant the most to us. The competency piece is simply the price of admission. You felt a connection, and chances are you worked harder for them.

||||||||||||||||||||||||||||||||||||||||||||||||||||||||||||||||||||||||||||||||||||||||||||||||||||||||||||||||||||||||||||||

What Makes a Great Boss or Colleague?

Do the following exercise and see what you learn:

1. Think of five people who have been influential in your career. They can be supervisors, colleagues, or mentors. Whom would you go and work with again, in a heartbeat, if given the opportunity?

2. List five qualities to describe each of them.
3. Go back and divide the qualities into two categories: "Competence" or "Connection." Competence refers to hard skills, such as intellect or functional expertise. Connection refers to social skills, like emotional intelligence, empathy, or shared values.
4. What is the ratio of Competence to Connection? Do you notice a pattern?

We Like Human Beings . . . and Other Lessons from Politics

Much of the country looks at politics as a warning for what not to do, but as a former political campaign insider, it taught me how people form connections with others in the toughest of circumstances. Think about it. Many voters are mistrustful of the candidates seeking elected office. There is negative information swirling continuously; personal attacks are commonplace. Voters rarely meet the candidate personally, thereby negating the most reliable means of establishing trust.

The only chance political candidates have is if voters feel a connection to them and grant them their trust (and then their vote). It boils down to the human component, which is told through the story of the candidate.

When I worked in politics, I was part of the creative team for a political consulting firm that developed print ads and direct mail messages for candidates. Each election year we represented about 50 candidates competing in everything from U.S. presidential to statewide campaigns. Our firm's process was like all the others in the industry. When we got a new candidate, we would learn all the compelling points about her: professional history, family life, personal story, challenges, and successes. Usually we also had polling data showing voter opinion on general issues, the candidate's positions on those issues, and her personal attributes. We would also read through a very thick book of research on her opponent ("Opp research") that detailed all of his negatives and weaknesses: tax liens, lawsuits, sketchy business dealings, untoward associates, fabricated or incendiary public statements, issues with educational background, and personal malfeasance. (When we were lucky, there was so much research it ended up being two thick books.) We would take all of this information and go into a closed-door meeting for hours—sometimes over the course of days—and pore over the details of our candidate's life and the political environment in her district.

We were keenly aware that in another room just like ours, our opponent's political consultants were going through a similar process, with their own research book about our candidate.

Our job was to create a strong individual connection between voters and our candidate. We had to find links so compelling that even a barrage of negative attack ads couldn't sever it. So what did we do? We looked for a blend of competency with vulnerability in the candidate's story. Political advisers do extensive polling throughout a campaign on their candidate's positives and negatives to see which ones land with voters. We had actual, hard statistical data about what voters liked about the candidate to back up our messages. Time after time, it was the candidate's connection on a deeper, human level that polled best with voters.

We developed messages about a candidate's rags-to-riches background, or her ability to build a business from nothing. We wrote ads about her strong family roots in the community through PTA and charitable endeavors. We preemptively exposed struggles the candidate had experienced, and how she overcame them through perseverance.

We turned a face on a campaign sign into a human being you'd invite into your home.

And we knew that a perfect history did not translate into a perfect campaign. The perfect candidates were the absolute hardest. Someone who's had it too easy doesn't sit well with voters. A perfect childhood, a prominent family, and a skyrocketing career were a recipe for voter apathy. There was nothing to hold on to. Voters needed to see that their leader was like them, a real person who works hard, has some trials along the way, and learns how to rise to the occasion. That's what creates a compelling presence.

You're the Only One Who Believes You Can Be Perfect Anyway

Hand in hand with the "all business" persona is the perfectionist. This is a challenge, especially for all you Type A personalities out there (yes, that means me, too). In an effort to be great, we try to get everything right: right people in the right jobs with the right outcomes. Many of us layer in the right personal life, the right accoutrements, and the right attitude. Everyone expresses it differently. But the end result is that the presentation of ourselves leaves out many of the challenges we face along the way, in an effort to show our best selves—all the time. We make the mistake of thinking that being open to feedback and admitting mistakes (or, God forbid, that we don't know something) is a damaging sign of weakness.

We equate being open with weakness when it's actually a sign of strength.

You probably know where this is going because even if the picture I've painted isn't you, you've met someone who fits the description. Like I mentioned before, perfectionism may get you admiration or even flat-out respect. But it will never get you the connection that renders it possible for someone to come into your office and tell you something you really need to know, despite the fact that it's difficult to say.

The funny thing about perfectionism is that while we may endeavor to embrace it in ourselves, no one else buys it. They can see right through it. They know when your confidence is actually just boasting, or how that catch in your voice reveals insecurity, or how your ever-present right answers don't always turn out so right in the end. Perfection creates the opposite of connection. One person's perfectionism causes guardedness in others. It sabotages openness, which is precisely the quality that gives us tremendous comfort in our leaders and colleagues.

A Case Study in Perfectionism: Boards of Directors Weigh In

One of my niches in executive coaching is working with first-time CEOs. As you might expect, they range from brilliant young technologists to experienced leaders who have successfully navigated corporate bureaucracies before now running a company.

I begin these engagements by talking to executives and employees who work with my client. In the case of the CEO, that includes the board of directors. A nearly universal dynamic occurs in these conversations: One of the presenting issues is commonly the CEO's relationship with the board itself. This issue encompasses communications around progress and mistakes, how to manage the board effectively, ways to address issues, and how to allow the board access to other senior team members without undermining the CEO's authority. CEOs want to appear confident and communicate clearly with their boards. They are concerned about having the board's buy-in to their ideas. In sum, CEOs want to know how to be more polished (read: perfect) in how they interact with the board.

Of all the board members I've spoken with over the years, only one has ever mentioned a desire for the CEO to communicate to the board in a more polished way, and that was an extreme case where the leader exhibited symptoms of adult ADHD. The board's concern is nearly always about trust and connection between the CEO and the board itself and the larger company. When a CEO seems too perfect, board members worry. When they hear only good news, they worry more. I often hear from board members who are concerned that the CEO doesn't seem open enough to feedback or that he has "an answer for everything." They typically sit on the boards of several companies and have often run businesses themselves. They know how messy companies can get. They want CEOs who can be honest, admit mistakes, and persevere in times of conflict. They want CEOs who know how to ask their board members for help. Yes, they want competence, but they also want vulnerability. After all, that's what board members trust on a human level.

Michael Dering serves on the boards of directors for eight companies. He's also a private investor who has been a successful CEO of both publicly and privately owned businesses. He led his last company, Service Bench, to a lucrative acquisition. He's seen the situation from all sides and put it this way in an interview for the book: "I look for CEOs who I'd like to be in the trenches with. Business is unpredictable and markets move fast. A good CEO actively confronts reality. The best CEOs know what they don't know and aren't afraid to ask for help anywhere they can get it, especially from their board.

"I expect the CEO to have an informed opinion, but not all the answers. No one does," he added.

If this dynamic is true among our highest levels of political and corporate leadership, you can bet it's just as true for the rest of us.

||||||||||||||||||||||||||||||||||||||||||||||||||||||||||||||||||||||||||||||||||||||||||||||||||||

Is Perfectionism Undermining You?

Write down the answers to the following questions:

- What perceived weaknesses or challenges about yourself are you holding back—to try to appear more perfect—that might create a connection point with others?
- Are there struggles or failures that you hide or routinely downplay?
- What could you reveal about yourself that would help others understand who you authentically are?

||||||||||||||||||||||||||||||||||||||||||||||||||||||||||||||||||||||||||||||||||||||||||||||||||||

You Can Be Open Without Opening Pandora's Box

Exposing the right amount of your vulnerable self without appearing weak or ineffective can be challenging. As I mentioned in the book's Introduction, I struggled considerably with this issue when I was running my company. In the early years, I overcompensated for my lack of experience by putting the perfection mask on pretty thick. I paid for it, too. In our first few years in business we had a soaring growth trajectory. Our main hurdle was building infrastructure and hiring staff fast enough. About two years in, we began having turnover problems. We brought in a coach to do a cultural assessment that included rating the company's leadership. My scores were the lowest. One particularly tough message: I wasn't considered a team player. How could that be? As the owner of the company, the team's fate and mine were intertwined. I was working my butt off to build a team and keep it together!

With the help of a coach, I learned to see myself through the eyes of my team. I was singularly focused on growing and stabilizing the business and was often engrossed in work. My workload felt tremendous, and eliminating distractions was my strategy for sanity. Team development was a lesser priority. I kept many of my thought processes to myself; as a result, people didn't feel as if they knew me well. Openness never came easy for me. "Reserved" is a term I've often heard to describe me.

Though the feedback was tough, I learned from it, because two of my signature strengths are learning and focus. Remember that pregame ritual that I outlined in Chapter 3? I was religious about using the time before our business development meetings to connect with my team and learn everything I could about them—and to be open to their questions in return. This was how I tried to overcome an aspect of myself that's hardwired.

One other important lesson I learned from that experience: Our company did not have a culture of feedback, although I thought we did. We gave plenty of top-down feedback in performance reviews. Positive feedback flowed somewhat readily. But we didn't make it a regular part of our daily work to give positive and negative feedback from the bottom up, colleague-to-colleague, or in the moment.

We needed to open up our communication channels so that we could gauge our performance. Certainly if I had grasped that idea back then, I would have been a better leader in those early years. (And I'm sure some of my staff would have loved to give the feedback!)

If you create a personal culture of feedback, often others will follow your lead.

This type of feedback represents a culture change, but it's not hard to do. You don't need to be running the company to incorporate this practice into your work life. Anyone can deliver quick feedback points (QFPs). QFPs are situation-specific, in-the-moment requests for feedback. Once you start, everyone will embrace this type of feedback. QFPs will spread virally throughout the organization.

You can ask for QFPs in any way that works. I like to ask: *What went well? What could I do better for next time?* It's a simple way to debrief after key events and demonstrates that you are willing to be open and learn, and that everyone has ideas to contribute no matter what their level, title, or history with the organization.

Your Stories Tell Your Story

The story I just told sums up the point I'm trying to make in this chapter. From it, you learned that I struggle. In no way do I think that I have this thing licked. I work hard and try to improve. And the telling of my story requires me to let down my guard and admit that I wasn't the perfect boss. It would be easier for me to talk about my achievements—believe me, *much* easier—but that wouldn't help you see that we all wrestle with many of the same issues.

Stories have a profound effect on humans. We are drawn to storytelling as a way to understand one another. We retain stories longer and more completely than facts and figures. Our minds understand stories on a deeper level. You know how you can hear a song and it takes you back to a certain place? Same thing with a story: When we are reminded of one part of a story we've heard, we are likely to remember the entire story. We are collectors of stories that we've lived or heard. From these stories, we've learned valuable lessons and created the morals and values that guide our actions. We hear stories, retell them, share them, and compare them to our own experiences.

Stories also affect the way we listen. When I deliver workshops I intersperse stories to illustrate my points. And I can see the effect on other people. As I launch into a story, people who have been looking down suddenly look up. Faces soften and shoulders relax. People sit back in their chairs. Smiles pop up. I can present the most impressive statistics, but it won't have that same effect. Only stories make people want to listen and absorb on that basic human level. The next time you have to present to a group, try to include a story and watch what happens. It's no wonder that we retain so much more information from stories.

> *Stories affect the way we understand, remember, and even listen.*

Storytelling has developed into a business art form as scores of books, articles, and training programs have arisen about how to be a more effective storyteller. There are even storytelling festivals, global storytelling days, storytelling conferences—you name it. If you are interested in becoming a better storyteller, there are countless avenues to pursue.

If you're pressed for time, you need not go to great lengths to learn basic storytelling skills. I bet you already know how to tell fascinating stories to your friends and family. Problem is, stories often get lost between our home and our workplace. As part of the all-business culture, we often believe that it's inappropriate to bring so much of our personal lives into the office. Many people assume no one else would care about their stories. Yet stories are the most direct way for people to understand what we're really about. They reveal the actions we've taken in the past, which is another powerful way of demonstrating our true presence. There's certainly a line between what's appropriate and inappropriate to discuss at work. Yet, having experienced some great storytellers, I know that there is greater latitude than most people think.

Stories serve multiple purposes in strengthening communications and presence. Consider adding stories to your communications when you:

— Want to motivate others and paint a picture of what's possible

— Need to show others—whether a large audience or one person—that you have shared commonalities

— Are trying to deliver difficult news and want to show empathy

— Are facing adversity in the present that relates to a situation you've experienced before

— Are interviewing for a job and want to demonstrate your ability to adapt, learn, and overcome challenges

— Are in a new position and would like to show others your approach and values

— Want to show clients or colleagues that you've been in their shoes

— Want to encourage another person to tackle something difficult

There's no right way to tell a story, but there are best practices. Here are some guidelines for incorporating more stories into your communication:

A good story . . .

— Has a clear moral or purpose

— Has a personal connection to the storyteller and/or the audience

— Includes common reference points the audience can understand

— Involves detailed characters and imagery

— Reveals conflict, vulnerability, or achievement others can *relate* to

— Has pacing (a beginning, ending, and segue back to the topic)

— Serves to strategically underscore your intention (it's not randomly told)

Be careful not to . . .

— Share only stories of your successes or hold back the parts that seem unimpressive. This quickly sounds like bragging.

— Ramble on. A good story should take one or two minutes, tops.

— Stray too far from the point. Meandering side stories will cause you to lose your audience. When you see fading eye contact or fidgeting bodies, speed it up.

— Share stories that could make some people in your audience uncomfortable or feel out of the loop. Frame your comments for the folks least likely to get it, not the ones most likely.

Our stories help define us, and they teach us. They are easier to communicate than most other information; they naturally put us at ease when we tell them (no memorization required); and they're easy for others to recall. Whether you are interviewing for your first job and want to show what you're made of, or you're a CEO trying to galvanize a company to climb the next big mountain, the right story will make it easier. The trick is to remember to use them. Once you make a habit of sharing stories, you'll get all the reinforcement you need to keep going.

One Extreme Case as a Cautionary Tale

I'm going to end this chapter with a client situation I found myself in a few years back. It's an extreme case, yet it offers a cautionary tale of what can happen when connection is startlingly absent.

For this engagement, I was brought into a government agency for a short training program to help the members of a senior team communicate more effectively with one another. When I went in to meet them, I experienced the perfect storm of every what-not-to-do in this chapter. From the moment I walked through the door, I could see that the team's culture was extremely guarded. The team members were seated around the table; their body language was closed and the air was thick with cautiousness bordering on suspicion. When I asked the group to speak about team communications, each person was quick to list all their best attributes, yet no one wanted to expose a weakness.

Besides one new woman, who seemed distressed, everyone on the team had been there for a decade or more, with some topping 20 years. Yet when asked, they admitted how little they knew about one another. Few talked about their families or outside interests. They didn't know where their coworkers commuted from or what brought them to their position. When I suggested an exercise where they discuss simple weekend plans, there was literally a collective sucking in of breath in the room. One man said pointedly, "We don't think it's appropriate to discuss our personal lives at work." When I began to discuss connection and storytelling, only the new woman spoke up to affirm the need to bring that kind of communication into the workplace. Everyone else in the room sat in dead silence.

You may be wondering how you can solve a problem that no one acknowledges. Well, it was impossible. I was only there for 90 minutes, and they were 90 *long* minutes. Because there wasn't a willingness to be open to feedback and to seek the humanity in others, there was no connection anywhere. The individuals had no connection to me, and no connection to one another. Underscoring all of it was a supreme lack of trust (which is the topic of Chapter 6).

And, by the way, I should add that the reason I was brought in was because of low employee morale in the department that reported to this senior team. I bet you could have guessed that.

Key Takeaways from Chapter 5

1. People like to work with people they like. When you forge true, authentic connections in the workplace, you'll be in on the critical information flow and countless opportunities.
2. Leaders especially must be vigilant to remain approachable and connected to their team or they may find themselves in a "toxic

tandem," where they are out of the loop precisely when they need to be in it the most.

3. Connection enhances presence when you reveal your competency alongside your vulnerability. It shows that you are human, just like the rest of us.

4. Perfectionism alienates others and creates a barrier to openness. By showing that you are open to feedback and can learn from mistakes, you actually demonstrate self-assurance and strength.

5. We seek out stories in others that show their humanity. Notice how political campaigns position their candidates. Whether it's overcoming a tough upbringing, surviving a war, or fighting cancer, a candidate's ability to face adversity makes him more likable and real to voters.

6. Make an effort to incorporate storytelling in your communications at work. Stories create shared meaning, are memorable, and define our characters. They're also enjoyable to tell.

Ideas I Want to Try from Chapter 5:

_____

_____

_____

_____

_____

_____

CHAPTER 6

Trust: The Ultimate Gatekeeper

The striking client story that I shared at the end of Chapter 5 shows what happens when trust is absent in a work environment. The reality for most of us is that trust is rarely so binary. We trust some people some of the time about some things, and the same is likely true for how others feel about us. Most of us go through the day without thinking much about our trustworthiness. We take it at face value. It's part of who we are, and we expect people to find us as full of integrity as we find ourselves. After all, we know our own motivations.

You may even wonder what trust has to do with presence. The short answer is: everything. Without trust, our guards stay firmly in the up position and true connections aren't made. And while our own trustworthiness might not be top of mind, we are consummate trust assessors of others. We carry our own trust meters and use them to rate others on what we value personally, so then we know how far to let them in.

> *What does trust have to do with presence? Everything.*

|||||||||||||||||||||||||||||||||||||||||||||||||||||||||||||||||||||||||||||||||||||||||||||||||||||||

What Items Are on Your Trust Meter?

While we may experience trust similarly, what makes someone trust-worthy varies based on our individual values and the qualities we weigh the most. Write down the qualities you associate with trust. Don't over-think it; just write what comes to mind.

|||||||||||||||||||||||||||||||||||||||||||||||||||||||||||||||||||||||||||||||||||||||||||||||||||||||

Trust is foundational to presence. That's because you need other people to feel comfortable enough about your motives and credibility to invest in you as a person. The more trust, the larger the investment. And if you are deemed untrustworthy, you'll have the opposite of investment—distance, suspicion, even sabotage.

The more trust others have of you, the larger their investment in you.

To extend the metaphor, if intention is your aim and connection your target, then trust is the atmosphere that carries your presence from Point A to Point B. Solid trust means clear skies, low wind, and a graceful landing. Lack of trust equates to rain and headwinds that knock your presence off course (or out of the game entirely).

Trust is a big concept. It's complicated because it's partly fact-based and partly emotional. We also have different trust standards for the workplace than we do in our personal lives. We tolerate more gray area around trust at work because we don't always expect as much from people in the workplace. It's assumed that leaders may act in their own self-interest or that ambitious colleagues will use others to get ahead. And getting a handle on our own general trust-worthiness is tougher still.

Yet trust is yearned for in the workplace. When we meet people we can fully and totally trust in our work lives, we feel a sense of se-curity and partnership. We also enjoy work more. Trust fosters friendships. Companies that report a large number of people re-sponding "yes" in employee surveys to the statement "I have a best friend at work" have more engaged employees and profitable busi-nesses, according to the Gallup Organization's research.[1] Whatever the norms or expectations may be in your organization, if you demonstrate that you are worthy of trust, you'll have greater connections and more fulfilling relationships. You'll have a presence that others seek out.

My goal with this chapter is to get you to think about your own trustworthiness first and foremost, and to realize that it is critical to a strong presence. I'm going to share some of the research that I've found helpful around what creates trust so that you can decide how you can augment your trustworthiness. For me, work on trustworthiness is most helpful as it applies to individual relationships rather than a faceless collective. I encourage you, as you read through this chapter, to think of an example of a relationship that could benefit from greater trust, more connection, or a stronger presence on your part. By working on trust as an individual endeavor, you'll find that your overall trustworthiness rises along with it. With trust, your actions definitely do speak volumes.

What Creates Trust and What Squashes It Like a Bug?

Several years ago, I was introduced to the work of David H. Maister, Charles H. Green, and Robert M. Galford on building and maintaining trust in professional services firms. Their ideas were published in a book called *The Trusted Advisor,* which quickly became a must-read for anyone working in a client service environment.[2] They do a momentous job of distilling a nuanced quality like trust into discernable actions that anyone can take. Their book validated my own approach to sales and client service over the years. And it exposed my culpability in relationships that didn't go as well as I had hoped.

Most of all, what I find interesting about their framework is that it applies to nearly any work relationship you can envision. We're all trusted advisers who rely on the strengths of our relationships to get things done. Influence has replaced hierarchy as a means to an end. Buy-in is not simply a nice-to-have. We have internal clients even if we never meet any external ones.

For this chapter, I am using their work liberally as an approach for building trust no matter your position, level, or work environment. Try it on for size in your world. I'm confident you'll see that it fits.

What Does a Trusted Relationship Look Like?

Maister et al. describe a set of traits that people whom we trust have in common. Do these traits ring true for you? Trusted advisers:

— Seem to understand us, effortlessly, and like us
— Are consistent (we can depend on them)
— Always help us see things from a fresh perspective
— Don't try to force things on us
— Help us think things through (it's our decision)
— Don't substitute their judgment for ours
— Don't panic or get overemotional (they stay calm)
— Help us *think* and separate our logic from our emotion
— Criticize and correct us gently and lovingly
— Don't pull their punches (we can rely on them to tell us the truth)
— Are in it for the long haul (the relationship is more important than the current issue)
— Give us reasoning (to help us think things through), not just their conclusions
— Give us options, increase our understanding of those options, give us their recommendation, and let us choose
— Challenge our assumptions (to help us uncover the false assumptions we've been working under)
— Make us feel comfortable and casual personally (although they take our issues seriously)
— Come across like real people, not like they are acting in a role
— Are reliably on our side and always seem to have our interests at heart
— Remember everything we ever said (without notes)
— Are always honorable (they don't gossip about others, and we trust their values)
— Help us put our issues in context, often through the use of metaphors, stories, and anecdotes (few problems are completely unique)
— Have a sense of humor to defuse (our) tension in tough situations
— Are smart (sometimes in ways we're not)

You may be nodding as you read these traits and behaviors. It can invoke a sense of calm just to think about these qualities. Often you can put a face to a description of someone who has been a trusted adviser in your life. Would others use these same descriptors for you?

Core Variables of Trust: The Trust Equation

The model outlined by Maister et al. in *The Trusted Advisor* is the "trust equation," which is a veritable road map for building connections and influence in an authentic way (see Figure 6-1).

$$Trust = \frac{Credibility + Reliability + Intimacy}{Self\text{-}Orientation}$$

Figure 6-1. The trust equation.

SOURCE: David H. Maister, Charles H. Green, and Robert M. Galford, *The Trusted Advisor* (New York: First Touchstone, 2000) p. 69.

Let's take the trust equation apart and briefly look at what the variables mean in our day-to-day experiences.

Credibility is in the realm of words. It's about our content expertise and presentation of our knowledge. When we study hard-to-learn facts and figures before a big meeting, we are working on our credibility. It's also about the academic degrees and the relevant experience a person has. It's often where professionals focus the most because our society values accumulated knowledge and having the right answers. Credibility feels safe because it's the most rational piece of the trust equation.

Reliability is in the realm of actions. It's about whether you can be trusted to deliver the same way and at the same level over a period of time. Reliability is enhanced by increased positive interactions. The more someone sees us behave in an expected way, the easier it is to trust us as a reliable presence. One-off performances that wow us don't carry nearly the weight of being consistent over time. This is why it's critical for leaders to actively engage with their teams regularly rather than waiting for big events. We get a high score on reliability when our actions have shown that we do what we say we're going to do.

Intimacy is in the realm of emotions. You probably found credibility and reliability to be fairly predictable. But when intimacy enters the room, things get shaken up. Intimacy is a tough concept to grasp in the workplace. We've become accustomed to (and comfortable with) keeping a professional distance in our interactions. It's the all-business persona I discussed in Chapter 5. Yet our trusted relationships always include a level of intimacy. We have to be able to open up— and encourage others to open up as well—or the real issues will never surface. In discussions with those whom we trust, we use candor and full disclosure because we know in this trusted relationship we'll be handled as friends and confidantes. Perhaps just as important, we also know that appropriate boundaries will be respected; therefore intimacy will be used to deal with the issue on the table, not to exploit the relationship.

Self-orientation is in the realm of motives. In the trust equation, it holds great power as the sole denominator. In my experience, this is exactly as it should be. When we perceive that people are putting their own motives above our own, we shut them out emotionally. Think of salespeople who will do and say anything to sell you their product.

When we see self-interest coming we mentally go the other way.

When you can see them coming, you run the other way (mentally, if not physically). Self-orientation is more than just selfishness. It's being overly fixated on ourselves in every situation; it's about our needing to look intelligent, have the right answer, push our agenda, or win at any cost. When trust relationships break down at work—or never get off the ground—self-orientation is often the culprit.

Can You Measure Trust? (Give It a Try)

Maister et al. propose that trust can be measured like a scored equation. They suggest that you give yourself a rating of 1 to 10 on each variable of trust—credibility, reliability, intimacy, and self-orientation—then do the math and see what you get. In their examples used to benchmark trust scores, a 5 equates to a long-standing trustful relationship while a 1.25 is a low trust score. As an absolute number, this trust score may or may not be useful to you. However, on a comparative basis—using separate relationships or with the same person over time—it can be enlightening.

||||||||||||||||||||||||||||||||||||||||||||||||||||||||||||||||||||||||||||||||||||||||||||||||

Calculate Your Trust Score

Do the trust equation for a specific relationship you'd like to strengthen. Give yourself a rating of 1 to 10 on the four trust variables (credibility, reliability, intimacy, and self-orientation) and then calculate your score using the equation in Figure 6-1.

How do you measure up? What variable can you enhance today?

||||||||||||||||||||||||||||||||||||||||||||||||||||||||||||||||||||||||||||||||||||||||||||||||

Sold on Trust, Where Do I Begin?

I've found that in tough relationships I can be lacking on a number of trust variables. That said, there are a few themes that come up routinely in my work with executive presence.

First, pay very close attention to your self-orientation. And I mean your true, authentic, deep self-orientation. It would be possible to write an entire chapter on managing self-orientation; as a coach, I see this issue come up a lot. To manage your self-orientation, you'll first need to understand it. Generally, well-intentioned people do not go into relationships trying to be selfishly motivated. It happens because we're human and

> *Self-orientation and intimacy have a ricocheting effect back and forth—either positively or negatively.*

there's so much at stake in our careers. Self-orientation is often a defense mechanism meant to protect ourselves against embarrassment, discomfort, failure, or even at times employee litigation. We have our own backs. And while it's natural and at times judicious to feel this way, it's also more transparent than we realize.

Self-orientation also has a "ricochet effect" with intimacy. We can't be open because we don't trust the other person's motives. Or they hold things so close to the vest that we make sure to protect our own interests. And so it goes: back and forth, again and again—confirming and reconfirming our initial opinions.

One way to stop this dynamic and lower the impact of self-orientation in a relationship is to take a step back and ask yourself:

> *What could I do for the sake of the relationship that would help the other person, even if it's against my own self-interest?*

Someone has to take the risk first. And since you're reading this book on presence, that someone can be you. You may worry about extending yourself, but as the old saying goes, "If you always do what you've always done, then you'll always get what you've always gotten." One person in a relationship has to be willing to take a step for the dynamic to improve.

Acts of selflessness can transform a relationship. Think of a leader who forgoes her bonus to make sure other people get theirs, or a sales guy who tells you sincerely that you don't need to upgrade this version of his product, or a manager who needs you but offers to advance your career to his own detriment. Acts such as these bring down walls and bust open doors. When they occur, you immediately reorient yourself toward the other person.

This extends not just to specific relationships you'd like to improve, but also to your relationship to others as a whole. It comes down to how you conduct yourself no matter the circumstances; in other words, your internal compass. Leaders who oversee teams of people can choose to orient themselves as a trusting/trustworthy person through a combination of their own presence and what they expect of others.

If we expect trust, we'll get it. If we expect a lack of trust, we'll get it.

There's a Pygmalion effect at play: The research shows that people rise or fall to their leader's expectations.[3] To a large extent, if we expect others to be trustworthy and to act in a trusting manner, they will. If we expect them to take advantage, they will.

For all professionals, there are times when a lot is at stake and it feels safer to operate from a place of self-protection than a place of trust. It doesn't matter whether you are dealing with clients or coworkers. You have a choice to make about the presence you want to convey. Extend trust or not? Invest in the relationship or keep your distance? These small interactions have a cumulative effect on your presence as a whole.

Sometimes we find ourselves stuck in a relationship that's not working. A common one is when the supervisor-employee dynamic has been damaged. Often, the people involved believe they have tried everything and yet the situation remains unchanged. Self-orientation—and mistrust—rises with each interaction. When you feel that you don't know what to do next and the relationship is still important to you, ask yourself:

What action would I take if I knew it would be accepted and appreciated?

This question will reveal the myriad options that are still available. That's because when we attempt to eliminate risk, we self-censor actions that have *any* chance of being rejected. But when you list all your options and consider each one's actual risk, there are usually quite a few trust-building moves on the table. And sometimes you have to mind your internal compass and do what you feel is right, no matter the outcome. (Which, by the way, reduces your self-orientation big-time.)

Situations Where Trust Is Hard to Come By (and Where to Find It)

So far we've discussed trust in abstract terms. We all experience situations where building and maintaining trust is tenuous. These are also times when we want our presence to support us, so it's important for our intentions and communications to be aligned. Focusing on strengthening trust in these tough situations not only helps you to get through them with less difficulty, but it helps you do so with grace and clarity.

Coming from a place of trust is a conscious decision. In every interaction, we can choose whom we want to be, and whether we will lead through our values or tuck them away in our back pockets. In the toughest of situations, we can be distracted into thinking that a Right Way prevails over our way because that's what worked for someone else, or because we're unsure of ourselves, or perhaps because well-meaning advisers recommended it. But the truth is, if you know what you value, you can usually find a path to effectiveness that supports whom you want to be. If you want to embolden trust, you have the ability. Here are my suggestions for how to keep trust high in typical work situations where it's a struggle. I call them "trust tester" situations.

Performance Issues

Everyone wants to do well at work; everyone wants the boss's approval. So when we have to let someone know that they aren't performing well, it's usually a difficult conversation. Most of the time, managers avoid these conversations so much that issues aren't addressed until they have ballooned into major problems.

It's best for all parties if the employee with the performance issue takes the feedback and improves. However, this won't happen without trust on both sides. Here are some ideas to consider for both parties:

Managers. Employees will want to know what this performance issue really means. Is it a small deficit or career limiting? Is this the first step before being let go? Have you already given up on them?

— Discuss the performance issue with as much candor as possible. Don't deliver feedback with so many caveats around it that the person has to read between the lines. Give the courtesy of specificity.

— Ask for the employee's perspective to ensure that you, as manager, understand the full situation.

— Show how you have managed performance issues in the past with others (maintaining confidentialities) and that you have a history of helping people to improve.

— Offer something that, while meaningful to the other person, is not in your self-interest—for example, regular one-on-ones, mentoring, cross-functional opportunities, or outside training.

— Check in regularly to show that you meant what you said and will be consistent.

— Continue to assess the employee's progress honestly, so there are no surprises.

Employees. Hearing that you are underperforming can provoke a knee-jerk, defensive reaction. Insecurity sets in. Your manager will be assessing how you take in the news and how you accept the feedback because it tells the manager a lot about the the attitude you'll be bringing to improving your performance—whether, for example, you'll be someone who can turn your performance around. You want to create trust so the manager knows that you're committed and can do it.

— Resist the urge to list all your accomplishments or to defend your work.
— Ask for complete honesty and gently push back if you feel you're not getting it.
— Extend an open invitation for the manager and anyone else to give you QFPs (quick feedback points) any time this performance issue comes up.
— Recap your understanding of the issue and what will happen next.
— Follow up by letting your manager know specifically what you'll be doing to address the performance issue with measurable benchmarks, if possible.
— State clearly to your manager how seriously you take the issue and your desire to improve.

Corporate Reorganizations or Layoffs

It only takes a rumor for trust to implode when corporate change is afoot, and even more so when it involves potential loss of jobs. Very suddenly those "in the know" are pitted against everyone else who is waiting to hear about their fate. Even positive change is generally difficult to handle. We resist it at our core, and as we now know from neuroscience, there's a biological basis. Our brains function most efficiently when we are working from the familiar.

When you are managing change on a team, or helping a company find its way through a reorganization, maintaining trust is crucial to sustaining performance, retention, and a positive culture. Try to:

— Establish the credibility of the leaders (including yourself, if applicable) who are shepherding the change process.
— Make reference to other, similar companies that have faced the same obstacles and pulled through. Keep a focus on what's possible on the other side.
— Avoid overpromising or creating a false sense of security. If the situation is going to be uncomfortable and jobs will be lost, say so.
— Make the first cuts the deepest rather than continuing to trickle through layoffs. You want to avoid the proverbial waiting for the other shoe to drop, if at all possible.
— Show the sacrifices that top leaders are making personally.
— Encourage your team to ask for status reports at any time and promise to be as candid as possible. If you don't know an answer, be honest.
— Give people as much information as you can so they feel a sense of control. Show that their lives are more important to you than your short-term objectives.

Failure

No one wants to fail, and no one likes to admit to failure. Yet we all do fail at times, and we can all learn tremendously from our failures. When people fail and try to cover it up, they erode trust. Leaders often do this through omission—such as abandoning a failed program and never bringing it up again. Everyone falls prey to the "hope they don't notice" strategy at one time or another. But life has a way of exposing these failures eventually. So why not take advantage of the opportunity to increase your trust quotient by handling failure from a place of honesty and development?

— For leaders, it's okay to fail, just not to hide. When something doesn't work, bring it up, address what happened, and take accountability. Explain what you learned and state what's next.

— For everyone, don't wait for your failure to be called out. Take it up the ladder—along with your solutions for addressing the situation.

Competitive or Undermining Colleagues

We want to work in an environment where everyone gets along and contributes equally. But all too often corporations are set up to be extremely competitive, and there are fewer seats the closer you get to the top. Functional heads are frequently pitted against one another in a sort of psychic and physical endurance test to see who gets promoted. It's no surprise that relationships between people who need each other to get things done can turn toxic when it feels like a zero-sum game. This situation is miserable for all parties and produces significant stress. Ironically, teamwork is one of the key skills required for promotion. So whether the friction is with a peer or a colleague in an entirely different position, it's in everyone's best interest to find a way to, as Rodney King so famously put it, "all just get along." You may never be able to singlehandedly morph a relationship, but you can do your part to enhance trust. How to start?

— Make it a mission to learn about your colleagues' motivations. The more you know about what makes them tick, the more context you'll have for understanding their behavior.
— Share your perceptions in a nonthreatening way. Use "I" statements rather than "You" statements. For example: "I'm picking up on some tension. I'd like for us to find a way for us to work better together. What can I do to make this work?"
— Show your willingness to support your colleagues. Back them up in a meeting or call out their excellent performance. Talk up a colleague's project to others. Be genuine! Offer sincere compliments, not flattery.
— Encourage regular interaction. Find ways to work together one-on-one to increase the positive impressions you have of each other. Consider starting with a "How can we help each other" meeting.
— If you find your way to an honest dialogue, own up to your part and anything you've done to impair the relationship.

Take accountability—don't defend your actions as a reaction to what someone else did.

— Keep talking. As Susan Scott put it so well in *Fierce Conversations,* "The conversation *is* the relationship."[4]

Selling

There are multitudes of resources on how to establish trust in sales situations, and it's not hard to see why—we buy from those we trust. *The Trusted Advisor* has a good chunk of material devoted to this particular topic with numerous ideas to try. As an entrepreneur who has brought in business worth millions of dollars, here is the process I've adopted:

— Start with the other person (your prospect). Ask what the prospect is looking to get out of the sales call. Spend more time asking questions and listening than talking.

— Learn everything you can about your prospects—their hopes, fears, and motivations. Find as many authentic commonalities as possible, whether personal interests, family, colleges attended, or people you both know. This closes the distance between you.

— Don't spend a lot of time talking about your experience and credibility unless the prospect asks. Today, prospects do their own research online; if you aren't deemed credible you wouldn't be at the table.

— Use every exchange as a chance to demonstrate how you will act after the prospect becomes a customer.

— Talk to and treat prospects (and clients) as friends. Be equal parts informal and respectful.

— Be transparent. Welcome them to call anyone on your client list, whether or not you've given them as a formal reference.

— Never lie or overpromise. Tell clients what's in *their* best interest, not yours. If you are not offering the best solution, say so. You'd be surprised how often goodwill comes back around.

Getting Hired

When we're trying to get hired we are often circumspect in our interactions; we think it's better to be safe than sorry. There's a fine line between being memorable, yet not so far outside the norm that we're not a good cultural fit. Few people go into an interview feeling comfortable enough to be fully themselves. At the same time, we have to establish trust so that people will invest in us. To do that, we have to form intimacy and lower our self-orientation. We must let our personalities out and be authentic. Having hired many people over the years, I found the absolute worst interviews to be the ones where the interviewee is holding back any comment that isn't 100 percent positive, or is overly formal or seems to lack a personality. You don't get enough of a sense of the true person to establish trust. On the other hand, if you focus on building trust, you will find that both sides learn more during the interview. (After all, you may be the interviewee, but you are interviewing the company, too.) With that in mind, interviewees should:

— Ask the interviewer what she'll be focusing on; is this a general interview, and are there certain parts of your background she wants to explore? Come prepared with questions to ask.

— Find commonalities with the interviewer. Ask to meet other people on the team and do the same with them. Create an atmosphere that's conducive to asking candid questions on both sides.

— Avoid playing games. Be honest about what other job opportunities you have on the table and where they stand.

— Be authentic about your feelings. If you are happy to be there or have followed the company from afar, let them know. If you have reservations, put them on the table.

— Explain the challenges you have faced (if asked). Discuss them openly and describe what you learned. Don't say some version of "I've never had real challenges" or "My greatest weakness is working too hard."

— Realize that how you follow up is part of the interview process.

— Extend a favor that is solely for the company, with no expectation of a quid pro quo. Send over a sales lead, refer a candidate for another job there, or follow up with an article about a competitor or customer.

Employee Terminations

I saved this one for last because, well, terminations are hard no matter what you do. No one wants to lose his job. When it happens, it's often a surprise, even if it was fairly expected. When you are the person doing the firing, it can seem absurd to think that trust can be involved in such a situation. The difficulty is compounded because terminations are generally managed to mitigate legal risk: Say as little as possible, get the person out of the office quickly, and have them sign a severance document agreeing not to sue. Legal advice is based on treating the employee as if she can't be trusted (or that she has possible criminal intentions). Having 15 minutes to pack up your belongings and then being escorted to the door does not leave a person with warm and fuzzy feelings.

I'm not an attorney, and anything I can contribute should not be construed as legal advice. What I will say is that I've never been completely comfortable with how terminated employees are treated, or how I've been advised to treat them in my own companies. I've made it an interest of mine to hear how other companies have managed to terminate employees and still treat them in a respected and trusted way. I want to reiterate that I'm not talking about the true bad seeds out there. The majority of people who get terminated don't fall into the saboteur category. They aren't dangerously inept. They're simply well-intentioned folks in the wrong job or lacking a few key skills for success.

Treating people with trust is good on a basic human level, but there are business ramifications as well. It helps both the manager and the employee move on in a positive way. It negates some of the backlash from the people left behind who may feel defensive about how their former coworkers were treated. And it has even larger implications. When fired employees decide to sue a company, it's often because of how they were treated on the way out. Here are some approaches I've seen help people exit a company with dignity and with the chance of a softer landing:

— Give someone early notice if you feel her performance is leading to termination. Don't assume she will exploit the situation and stop doing her work entirely. Act as a mentor to help her find a more suitable role in another department or company, or encourage her to consider a new path.

— Offer to let the person resign on his own accord with two to three months of pay (either while continuing in the job or as severance).

— Hire the employee as a consultant on a part-time basis for a period of time to wrap up unfinished projects.

— Create a corporate policy of outplacement where terminated employees are given a desk and office as a base of operations or access to other resources.

— Make introductions to company recruiters who can locate a more suitable position for the person.

Finally, there's another side to terminations, which is the employee's approach and behavior. Nearly everyone will part ways with a company at some point—whether it's a for-cause termination or a layoff, or to voluntarily accept a better opportunity. Here's a universal truth that greatly impacts trust: People remember how you leave, more so than what you did before that. It may not be fair, but it's true. You have an opportunity to build trust and respect by being helpful, contributing your best to the last minute, refraining from spreading negativity, and working with the company to make the transition as smooth as possible for everyone. You may find these things difficult to do because, after all, you're leaving for a reason. Just remember that trust goes both ways, even in the toughest of circumstances. Business circles are small and your integrity and reputation are portable. Taking the high road is an investment in your future—even if you can't see it at the time.

We All Seek Out a Trusted Presence

Think of how often you seek out trusted colleagues for honest feedback or to bounce ideas off of. If you don't have trusted colleagues at work, I bet you don't like your job very much. Having people around us whom we trust is that important to overall happiness.

With trust, you reap what you sow. As you work on your presence, consider who presently counts you as a trusted

Show me someone who doesn't have a trusted friend at work, and I'll show you someone who doesn't like her job.

friend. Also ask yourself which of your relationships you would like to improve, and then make a move to extend trust in that broken dynamic. If not now, when?

Key Takeaways from Chapter 6

1. Trust is foundational to presence because you need others to feel secure about your credibility and motives so they invest in you as a person. The more trust, the larger the investment.
2. Trust can be measured and scored using the trust equation: Trust = (Credibility + Reliability + Intimacy) / Self-Orientation. This equation is a compelling tool to understand what's involved in creating and sustaining trust.
3. When relationships break down or never take hold, self-orientation is often to blame. Furthermore, self-orientation and intimacy play off each other to create a negative or positive spiral, depending on the weakness or strength of both.
4. If you want to be more trustworthy, then extend more trust to others. Just like in the Pygmalion effect, with trust, you get what you expect.
5. In trying situations at work, where presence can be hard to maintain, try to focus on trust building. By strengthening the elements of trust in a relationship, we also buttress our executive presence to manage with clarity and grace.

Ideas I Want to Try from Chapter 6:

_____

_____

_____

_____

_____

CHAPTER 7

What You Can Learn About Emotional Intelligence While Riding in the Elevator

Imagine you're at work, running to catch the elevator. It opens, and as the doors peel back you see that one of the top leaders at your company is already inside. You could experience either of the following reactions:

Oh crap, why didn't I push the button a few seconds later? It's going to be a painful ride filled with heavy silences wedged between awkward small talk.

Or:

Cool! I get to catch up and hear what's going on, from a company leader.

Most of us can relate to this type of experience. What accounts for the difference between the two scenarios, one cringe-worthy and one welcome? You might think the answer is the leader's basic social skills, and it's true, those certainly would help make for a more enjoyable ride with almost anyone in a 4-by-6-foot box. But social skills alone won't make a person excited to see the company's leader. I would argue that it is the leader's emotional intelligence, and more specifically, how connected and empathic the leader is, that makes all the difference between the responses.

Of course, another question to consider is: What's it like to ride an elevator with *you* as the leader?

The elevator example illustrates the distance that people can feel from their leaders. Some leaders feel very "other" to us, while some find a way to express commonality and sameness. It's not about being friends with direct reports, or being the person everyone wants at the party. Many leaders don't aspire to be the boss everyone socializes with after work. (Of course, some do, and that's fine as well.) The point isn't to become friends; it's to bridge the distance by making others feel comfortable enough to speak truthfully to you, and to feel a connection with you. The alternative? Discomfort leads to disconnection leads to disaffection. Not so good.

Empathy: The Killer App in Emotional Intelligence

Emotional intelligence is defined by John D. Mayer and Peter Salovey, two of the leading researchers on the topic, as "the ability to monitor one's own and others' feelings and emotions, to discriminate among them and to use this information to guide one's thinking and actions."[1] In our discussion of presence, leaders can go a long way toward emotional intelligence by simply understanding those around them better. Empathy, as the saying goes, is "the killer app."

In creating authentic connections, trust and empathy go hand in hand. If we don't feel that someone understands us, we are unlikely to forge a strong bond. In corporate America, the idea of the empathic leader has become a cultural prototype to which managers aspire. The theory that emotional intelligence, including empathy, is more important to leadership success than is intellectual acumen is widely accepted. In nearly every company, you can hear the term bandied about. "So and so lacks emotional intelligence" or "We don't have emotionally intelligent leadership here." We have Harvard-trained psychologist and former *New York Times* science journalist Daniel Goleman to thank for that. His mega-successful 1996 book, *Emotional Intelligence,* and multiple bestselling follow-ups, showed through extensive research that empathy is positively related to business success.[2]

While Goleman may have made the concept of emotional intelligence famous, it was a much lesser known psychologist named Dr. Reuven Bar-On who did the heavy lifting scientifically around the concept a decade earlier. Starting in the 1980s, Dr. Bar-On began studying a person's emotional quotient, or EQ. Eventually, he developed a statistically valid assessment tool called the BarOn EQ-i.[3] The EQ-i test (Emotional Quotient Inventory) has been taken by tens of thousands of leaders in nearly 40 countries to study characteristics that include empathy and interpersonal skills, as well as other factors such as adaptability, stress tolerance, and self-awareness. As a coach certified to administer the assessment, I believe that the findings can be powerful because the qualities measured are recognized to be vitally important. Who doesn't want to be more emotionally intelligent? These days it's hard to argue that empathy and connection aren't critical for leadership.

These are seminal leadership concepts, but I'm not going to use this book to sell you on the idea that emotional intelligence and social acumen are important to presence. I'm going to guess that by picking up this book (not to mention reading this far into it) you are already in that camp. I'd rather use this chapter to discuss what happens in real life between what we know we should do and what we actually do, or what we feel and what we express.

Most people agree that empathy is a valuable trait for leaders, but struggle with how to express it.

Empathy often falls directly through this knowing-doing gap. This chapter is about how to tap into your authentic empathic self and show it to others in the workplace in a way that enhances your presence and increases connection. When you break it down, it's simpler than you may think. Yet, it's a struggle for most of us, especially as leaders. As with so many other things, it's all in the execution.

Either Work Is Filled with Sociopaths or Empathy Is Hard to Communicate

On the one hand, the role of empathy in the workplace is so obvious it's comical. *Of course it's important to have empathy!* Unless you are born with sociopathic tendencies, you have natural empathy for others around you. It makes good sense that we relate better on a human level if we express empathy. On the other hand, in the leadership realm, expressing empathy in a company, on a team, or as part of a cross-functional project is fraught with difficulty. The lines are suddenly blurred between being understanding and being taken advantage of. We get hung up on how much emotional distance we should keep—how much we can invest personally without being sucked in. Sometimes it's just easier to be squarely dispassionate.

Leaders hold back expressing empathy for fear of being sucked in or taken advantage of.

Recently, I was speaking to a group of business owners about lessons learned in my work coaching CEOs. One of my points was that communicating respectfully to employees requires a CEO to manage his own emotional reactions. In the rush to market, equanimity may be sorely lacking in upstart companies. Employees need to feel that they'll be treated with dignity in order to take risks and perform over time. One example I gave to the business owners: Don't blast people in meetings for messing up, but handle performance issues in private. This wasn't groundbreaking content—just a reminder. I got about two-thirds through my point when one of the audience members boisterously offered that he completely disagreed. In his experience having run three companies, he said that people needed to be called out in front of their peers for their poor performance. After all, metrics were metrics. He said this raised the bar for everyone else. In fact, he claimed he used the public lambast strategy frequently as a motivational tool. I attempted to engage on my point and expound upon how his employees might view things, but I could tell by his body language that he wasn't hearing it. He believed his way was the right way, and that was that.

Your first reaction might be "What a jerk!" I'll be honest, it crossed my mind, too. (Okay, it more than crossed my mind. It hovered.) But there's more to it. Having observed both sides of this issue, I can see the interplay. On one side, I've been a leader and now sit in intimate talks with other leaders every day. I know that for many leaders, the most vexing, internalized issues are around how to better understand and manage their teams. It's an omnipresent topic in leadership coaching.

On the other side, I also regularly speak with employees (through the 360-degree process) about how their leaders function. As such, I hear the personal toll it takes on them when they perceive empathy to be absent. They have one foot out the door awaiting the final indignation. They look out for themselves. They aren't vested.

And I hear the reverse: When employees sense that their leaders get them as people, they'll forgive quite a bit on

> Employees will give more latitude to an empathetic leader.

the management side. So if leaders feel empathy but employees don't see it expressed, what gets in the way?

- *Time*. By far, time is the biggest culprit. Many leaders would love to understand their teams better or be more personally connected, but they don't have the time. Reaching out is time-intensive, and it simply falls to the bottom of the executive's daily list.
- *Personal Discomfort*. This empathy stuff is on the touchy-feely side of the continuum, and some leaders fear getting into an emotional conversation that's out of their comfort zone. It's better never to go near the personal side than to risk taking off someone's professional mask to find tears underneath. They're businesspeople, not psychotherapists.
- *Short-Term Thinking*. Leaders can choose to take an autocratic style that may work well in the short term. They know they're pushing their people too hard or managing too aggressively, but they plan to do something about it after the next hurdle (or the next one, or the one after that . . .).
- *Accidental Success*. I have a sneaking suspicion this was a factor at play with the man in the preceding story. Sometimes leaders accidentally get lucky, at one company or at one time, with a take-no-prisoners management style. I've seen this happen with entrepreneurial companies. When employees have a chance at cashing out substantial stock options, they can suck up anything. However, at some point, getting results from treating employees as merely a means to an end will reach a point of diminishing returns—and likely sooner than you think.
- *Few Open Communication Lines*. As discussed in Chapter 5, leaders find themselves distanced from the rest of the company right

when they need open communications the most. Leaders need constant data to formulate the "word on the street." This macro-sentiment can be even more helpful than individual comments because it's broad-based and less biased. When communication lines are closed, leaders don't know where to get accurate information if they want it, and no one is offering it up. If you are a leader, you need to hear straight from others what it's like to work for you.

There's More Than One Way to Empathize

For some, the phrase *empathic leadership* evokes images of group hugs, shared tears, and endless team-building sessions. Empathetic leaders might even seem like pushovers, or less ambitious. But if you've been lucky enough to work for an empathic leader, you know that they rarely come in this mold. In fact, they come in various shapes and sizes—just like anybody else. Only *you* can create the leadership style that fits your authentic self. Consider a few different styles of empathic leaders:

The Coach shows empathy through a mixture of tough love and strong support. The coach is not afraid to push you because she sees the best in you. This leader has a good sense of what's going on in the rest of your life and isn't afraid to mention it as it relates to your performance and potential.

The Mentor makes you feel that your success is always top of mind. Mentors have your back to guide you along in your career. They will act as a confidante as you hash through ideas and won't hold it against you as you iterate. Because they have done well, they operate from a point of helping others do the same.

The Truth Teller believes that you treat employees as adults and free agents who have a right to hear it straight. The truth teller doesn't sugarcoat as a matter of principle and can be counted on to let you know what you are doing well and where you can improve. You always know where you stand.

The Buddy eschews hierarchy as a structural imperative. The buddy seeks to be considered a colleague first and foremost. He's someone who stays in the trenches to keep a bead on the team, operating from the idea that "we're all in it together." The buddy leader frequently socializes with the team and can easily approach others with feedback as part of daily interactions.

The Relater has an intuitive ability to grasp the emotions of others. Whether from personal experience or keen observational skills, relaters tap into the hopes and fears of those around them and relate what they see to their own experience. They are self-revealing through shared stories. Even if you don't know them personally, you get the feeling that "they get you" in the abstract and that you know what they're about.

As you read through these prototypes for empathic leadership styles, you probably recognize one of these characteristics, or a blend of them, in yourself or in others. The examples are divergent in their styles, yet all seem like pretty great people to work for. No doubt you gravitate toward some of these leaders more than others, based on your own perspective. We all do.

Only you can create the leadership style that's authentic to who you are.

The best way to incorporate—and sustain—an empathic leadership style is to do it in a way that's authentic to you. You don't have to fit into the touchy-feely mold, or any of those I just described. There's wide latitude here. Keep an open mind about what empathic leadership means—the ability to understand and relate to the feelings of others—and you may find that there are behaviors that you can adopt quite naturally. One of the best places to start is by modeling the leaders who have inspired you in various aspects of your life.

For me, a resonant example of someone who embodies the exact right mix of empathetic, effective, results-focused leadership is Jim Kaitz, the CEO of the Association for Financial Professionals (AFP). The 15,000-member AFP is best known for its annual conference—billed as the largest annual meeting of corporate treasury and finance professionals in the United States—as well as for being a professional development resource and credentialing body for finance professionals.

Since Jim took the helm in 1998, he's been the driving force in expanding the organization from a treasury-focused niche association to a global finance thought-leader, nearly tripling revenue in the process. Some leaders achieve these kinds of results but leave a charred path behind them. Jim's style is decidedly different. He's a transformational leader who drives accountability and performance. People who work for Jim know that they need to bring their best to work every day. Jim is diligent and energetic and has a coveted ability to combine big-picture thinking with a clear understanding of the daily execution necessary to achieve it. Jim is not the boss to have if you want to slack off.

At the same time, Jim is one of the warmest and most empathetic human beings I know. He has fierce loyalty from his team, with retention numbers to back it up. I've heard from numerous people at AFP over the years that Jim is the reason they're in the job. Jim cares deeply about his people, and it shows through in everything he does—including being direct and straight with them. He doesn't placate or coddle; in fact, he's so transparent that his goals, and the goals of every single person working at AFP, are visible to the entire company. When asked to explain his magic formula, Jim is self-effacing and modest.

"I believe in people and thankfully that comes through," he explains. "It's my job to come to work every day and be an advocate to help others achieve a common goal. I inherently believe that people want to do a good job, and why wouldn't I want them to be successful? I make it clear that we'll all be held accountable, but at least we're in it together."

Jim prioritizes his position as a team champion. He knows that greatness will be accomplished through his ability to win hearts and minds. It's a role he accepts readily and with intention. "You have to absolutely commit yourself to the people side of this job. You build trust when people see that you genuinely care about them. If you claim to care and it's not perceived, you've lost. You can look people in the eye and say we have to do a better job here when they know you care. Threats never work in the long run."

Jim believes that empathetic leadership is stable leadership. "I was told a long time ago that I'm predictable, which I take as a compliment. If leaders show volatility and inconsistency people will play it safe around them. I want their best thinking. My team [members] know what they will get from me, even in times of controversy or stress. One of my favorite sayings is that self-awareness is a powerful tool."

Finally, he reinforces the point made earlier in Chapter 5: Exhibiting weakness alongside strength shows a leader's humanity and fosters trust. "Having people know who you are as a person is critical," he says. "You have to bare your soul a bit and be vulnerable or people don't feel comfortable with you as a person."

Empathy Outward Requires Empathy Inward

Another part of emotional intelligence that deserves to be discussed alongside empathy is the idea of self-management. On the BarOn EQ-i, it's discussed as "emotional self-awareness," or the ability to understand what emotion you are having while you're experiencing it. This sounds easy enough, except that humans aren't so good at it. We can be angry and not even know it until someone else calls us on it. Only then do we realize, hey, I am ticked off at what my coworker said yesterday. And sometimes we displace our emotions. Consider the proverbial "kicking the dog" syndrome.

When we don't stop to examine the genesis of our feelings, it's hard to control our impulses. We fly off the handle easily, or without even realizing it we take actions that are out of alignment with our intentions. That's why before we can express empathy toward others, we first must show it toward ourselves. Otherwise, our own stresses and emotional baggage will drag us down. After all, how can we put ourselves in someone else's head if we can't figure out how to manage our own emotions?

Here's a little background to illustrate this point: It's a dirty little secret that most entrepreneurs walk around with a hefty, at times crushing, sense of fear. Many businesses are just a few short steps from disaster at any given moment. Products can bomb, employees can sue, customers can refuse to pay, and funding can dry up. In fact, there are so many ways to fail, and fail spectacularly, that I began to see starting a business as the *opposite* of the easy path to the American

Dream. Thankfully, no one figures out how hard it is until they're in the middle of it, which explains why our entrepreneurial culture continues to flourish.

Fear of failure isn't even the hardest part. As a business owner, you are personally shouldering an enormous amount of risk. If you have employees, you are personally liable for payroll taxes, retirement savings, and possibly more, depending on how the business is structured. Your personal assets—mostly likely your home—guarantee debt and long-term liabilities. I vividly remember having dinner with a friend who was frustrated about his job and concerned his position might be at risk. "You're lucky," he said. "If you mess up, you won't lose your job." "No," I conceded. "But if I mess up, I could lose my business, my house, and lots of other people would lose their jobs." Touché.

If entrepreneurs can't learn to manage this fear it will bury them. You can't sell to new customers or motivate employees from a position of fear. You definitely can't innovate or encourage outside investment when fear is oozing from your pores. No one's personal presence intention is "gnawing dread" or "frenzied panic." Worse, fear is insidious—it masquerades as frustration or anger or stress. It can make you irritable and protective. Your only hope is to label it, make it explicit, and fight it face-to-face. A mentor of mine once told me when I was in a serious place of fear to remember that things are never as good or as bad as they seem. That became my common refrain when circumstances were particularly dicey. Remembering it helped me dampen the fear and regain perspective. It took a conscious effort to force self-reflection to manage the fear, sometimes using the techniques I discussed in Chapter 3 for tackling communications anxiety. It took me a while, but I came to understand that when I reacted so strongly to an issue I needed to take a step back and analyze where my reaction was actually coming from. I've spent my career around entrepreneurs, and I know with certainty that it's the same for most of us. Fear is a constant, and emotional self-awareness is necessary for survival.

And entrepreneurs are not alone. Lots of executives redirect anger, frustration, sadness, or fear without realizing it, undercutting their capability. Tempers flare, turf battles rage, words strike defensive chords, and stress pervades. In this kind of environment, simply knowing what's actually going on provides a strong defense against unconscious reaction. You can't manage what you don't know.

The next time you have an extreme reaction or feel anxiety or stress, ask yourself: *What's that about?*

After you answer, ask it again: *And what's that about?*

Keep going with the same line of questioning until you arrive at the true emotion underlying your action. Then tackle it.

You may find that when you extend a bit of empathy to yourself, it's a lot easier to extend it to others as well. At the very least, you'll have firmer, better-understood emotional ground from which to do the extending. Emotionally intelligent leadership sees destructive emotion for what it is, sets a positive intention, and works toward it.

It's Easy to Be Heavy, but Hard to Be Light

The author G. K. Chesterton first coined the phrase "It's easy to be heavy; hard to be light." I love the resonance for executive presence. Many leaders, and especially new ones, find themselves trying to create some distance from those around them. It's as if they need to go through a metamorphosis to redefine themselves as elevated versions of their former selves. In this new state, you'll make sure (in a new, to-be-determined way) that everyone knows who's boss. It will involve embodying some sort of commanding presence with just the right touch of superior attitude.

A lot of people fall into this trap, especially when promoted in the same organization. I recall talking through this issue with a mentor after I was promoted from team member to team manager. I was telling him all the things I was going to do so that everybody would know I was in charge. He simply said, "Kristi, everybody already knows you're the boss. You need to focus on how to make your team want you as their leader."

The distance comes naturally with any leadership position. It happens so quickly it can knock you back a few feet. You don't have to create it. What you *do* have to create is the presence to bridge that distance between you, as manager or leader, and others on your team. The individual connection has to be so strong that even as you arrive at a place where you can't possibly know everyone, everyone still feels as though they know you. I've never seen this happen by playing the heavy. It takes the empathy card to go the harder road and play it light.

Tony Hsieh, CEO of the hugely successful online retailer Zappos and a thought-leader on connected leadership, puts it this way: "If you think of the employees and culture as plants growing, I'm not trying to be the biggest plant for them to aspire to. I'm trying to architect the greenhouse where they can all flourish and grow."[4]

Become a Commonality-Finding Machine

A conversation I frequently have with clients I coach goes something like this:

Client: I'm having trouble with someone on my team. He's not performing as I need him to. I'm starting to see some push-back and frustration. I need to talk with him, but I want to approach it correctly. What should I do?

Me: What do you know about him? What motivates him?

Client: I'm not sure. He's hard to talk to. We don't have much in common. I don't know him very well. I know he's from California originally and had a kid last year. That's about it.

Me: Sounds like you don't know enough about him to manage him appropriately. Let's start there.

At the risk of presenting a scenario that seems glaringly obvious, I can't change the fact that this type of dynamic is common. It happens for all the reasons discussed in this chapter—lack of time, comfort level, or priority. Leaders have to try hard to find connection points and commonalities with their people, or they won't exist. It won't happen organically. Distance happens organically. And this information is vital, not only to an empathic leadership style or emotional intelligence but to effective motivation and management.

You can learn about your teams in as many ways as humans can communicate. That's pretty much why office happy hours and off-site gatherings exist. However, I'm a big fan of the Discovery Lunch. Meals get people out of the stuffy office and into a more relaxed setting. People let their guard down when a meal is shared. Consequently, we're primed to show a lighter, more personal side of ourselves. As the leader, your job at this lunch is not to discuss work or upcoming projects but to gain a fuller picture of the person sitting in front of you. Similar to the discovery phase in a legal engagement—though in a kinder, gentler fashion—you are finding answers. You can discuss home life, hobbies, anything you want. Just be sure to ask these two questions:

— What do you want for yourself and your career?
— How can I, and your position, help you achieve it?

If you know the answers, then you have potent information to lead another person. You know how to motivate people. You know how to retain them. You know what you can do to increase connection. You create commonality through shared goals.

In the best possible world, you want to start with new hires so that you can set the tone for your leadership style while the person has a fresh perspective. But Discovery Lunches work for existing teams, too. Be forewarned, though: If you spring it on people out of the blue and start asking lots of questions, they might be a teensy put off—and fear something fishy is about to happen. Make an announcement to your full team that you want to catch up with everyone, and that you'll be scheduling lunches with each person in a certain time frame. Once you initiate the idea, make it a quarterly occurrence.

Let's go back to that elevator ride. What if the leader knew two or three things he had in common with you? Then, instead of engaging in awkward chitchat, he could mention a sports team you both liked, or remark on the college you attended, or share a skiing story. It would have been a very different elevator ride.

To create connection, leaders need to be commonality-seeking machines. Every interaction is an opportunity to bridge the difference by seeking out areas that create sameness and understanding. Even if you lead a team of thousands of people around the globe, if you use distinct interactions to be inquisitive about others you'll build that individual connection. It enhances the interpersonal dynamic like nothing else.

||||||||||||||||||||||||||||||||||||||||||||||||||||||||||||||||||||||||||||||||||||||||||||||||||||||||||||||||||||||||||

The Zero Degrees of Separation Game

Write down the names of each of your direct reports. Can you name two or three things you have in common with them? (Working at the same company doesn't count! However, if you used to have a similar job to theirs, that does.)

How many people could you easily find common ground with?

For anyone you missed, you know what to ask next time you share an elevator.

||||||||||||||||||||||||||||||||||||||||||||||||||||||||||||||||||||||||||||||||||||||||||||||||||||||||||||||||||||||||||

The Virtuous Circle of Empathy

For many people, the concept of empathy is clear, but in the moment of an interpersonal exchange or a slight conflict, it becomes elusive. When you are faced with a situation that requires more demonstrable empathy than comes readily to you, it is helpful to have a strategy to fall back on, to prepare for your part in the discussion.

Being more empathetic boils down to being open, listening, and acknowledging what you hear. (For years I searched for something easier so that I might avoid the inevitable question: *You mean I have to spend more time listening?*) The most admired leadership scholars and authors have all covered it—Peter Drucker, Stephen R. Covey, Jim Kouzes and Barry Posner, Peter Senge, to name but a few.[5] The EQ-i emotional intelligence assessment offers an entire development section on ways to listen and

Empathy gets lost in the heat of the moment.

acknowledge others in a person's everyday work life. Nearly every executive communication book I've ever read (which is a lot, given my penchant for beating to death any topic I care about) mentions the same empathy strategies. In *Leadership Presence,* Belle Linda Halpern and Kathy Lubar lay out a straightforward and compelling case for how leaders can use the techniques honed by actors to empathize with anyone through listening, acknowledging, and sharing.[6]

Although the time-honored strategies are the ones that work, many of us have a hard time putting the pieces together in situations where empathic connections are especially critical. I've found it can be helpful to view empathic communications as a process. To that end, I use this virtuous circle of empathy, outlined in Figure 7-1, as a model. It can be used for tough conversations with employees, to get to the bottom of derailed projects with colleagues, or to help out a friend. It serves as a reminder to develop an executive presence that others consider open, considerate, and connected. The specific situation is irrelevant.

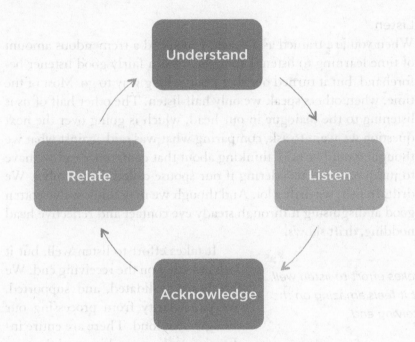

Figure 7-1. Virtuous circle of empathy.

Let's examine what the four boxes in Figure 7-1 mean in this context.

Understand

As the jumping-off point, understanding is the willingness to go into the conversation from a position of learning, not of knowing. It is the 5th habit of Stephen Covey's *7 Habits of Highly Effective People*: "Seek first to understand, then to be understood."[7] Your job is to understand everything you can about the person, the situation, the background—everything. Take a step back and ask yourself, "What if this person were me?" At some point, it may have actually *been* you. Consider yourself an information gatherer and collect feedback on the situation from various angles. Then in the discussion, ask questions of the other person in an attempt to paint a fuller picture. Don't assume you already see it.

Listen

When you are trained as a coach, you spend a tremendous amount of time learning to listen. I thought I was a fairly good listener beforehand, but it turned out that I had a long way to go. Most of the time, when others speak we only half-listen. The other half of us is listening to the dialogue in our head, which is going over the next question we want to ask, comparing what was said against what we thought would be said, thinking about that conference call we have to jump on next, wondering if our spouse called the plumber. We drift. In fact, we drift a lot. And though we may think we've gotten good at disguising it through steady eye contact and reflective head nodding, drift shows.

> *It takes effort to listen well, but it feels amazing on the receiving end.*

It takes effort to listen well, but it feels amazing on the receiving end. We feel heard, validated, and supported. We gain clarity from processing our thoughts out loud. There are entire industries, such as coaching and therapy, built around listening because it's so valued. To truly listen, you must be entirely present and focused on the full measure of the other person. Good listeners:

— Communicate with only the people in front of them (phones, email, and outside interruptions are ignored).
— Ask questions from a place of genuine curiosity, not to lead the other person to their agenda (accordingly, they use more *What* or *How* questions than *Why* questions).
— Focus on the other person's answers, not on their own thoughts.

— Probe in areas that seem important to the other person, not necessarily to them (e.g., *Tell me more about what concerns you with that* . . .).

— Aren't worried about being right or having a pithy reply.

— Notice the person's body language as a form of feedback.

— Observe their own body language to keep an open posture.

— Can take disparate answers and reflect back patterns.

— Are willing to flow with the conversation.

Acknowledge

Acknowledgment means verbalizing that you see the view the other person has from her seat. It's a validation of another person's position. Notice I didn't say that it's a validation of another person's position as *your* position. This is why acknowledgment can be difficult, especially when we patently disagree with the other person's perspective. Acknowledgment may look like acceptance, but it's not. Acknowledgment is not agreement. It's not even close.

> *Acknowledgment is neither acceptance nor agreement.*

It doesn't take much to show acknowledgment. It simply is letting someone know:

I can see why you would say that . . .

I understand where you're coming from . . .

I get that you are disappointed . . .

Of all the aspects of the virtuous circle of empathy, acknowledgment has the ability to completely change the conversation. It's like an "I'm sorry" when you are arguing with a loved one. Everyone takes a deep breath and some steam goes out of the fight. The problem is still discussed, but less confrontationally.

Acknowledgment has the ability to move two people at cross-purposes to the same purpose. It lowers defenses by demonstrating that you understand the other person's viewpoint. The other person's opinion is rational and valuable—even if it's not your own.

Relate

Relating is the last and most straightforward stop in the circle. It means comparing another person's experience to one that you've observed. For instance, if you are talking to colleagues about their struggle with a part of their job, you let them know that you've had a similar issue in the past—or that you've watched a colleague overcome the same thing. It need not be an exact comparison. As a matter of fact, it can be affirming to note that while you don't have direct experience of the particular situation, you are familiar with similar situations and share a common work ethic or approach. You get the point. By relating, you are bringing yourself into the discussion. Stories are a perfect vehicle to use here. When we relate to someone fully, it reinforces that we know what it feels like to walk in his shoes.

One caveat: While sharing your experiences is important, be mindful not to share too much. You don't want to hijack the conversation. If the conversation is becoming about you, find a way to steer it back to the other person.

Two Ways Empathic Leadership Plays Out

Demonstrating an empathic leadership style produces positive results in engagement, retention, motivation, and camaraderie. The benefits are hard to exaggerate. However, when situations get tenuous, that's when connected leadership can draw a line in the sand. Leaders who can bring that individual connection to their teams create transformational outcomes. They save companies, redefine purpose, and change lives. Here are two divergent examples of empathic leadership at work. The venues and the scales vary, yet you can see the virtuous cycle in both.

Example 1: Empathy Creating Possibilities

Kevin, a CEO of a management-consulting firm, was grappling with how to part ways with his managing director, Dana. For the past year, he had tried everything to improve Dana's performance. After much hand-wringing, he knew that she was simply not right for the job. She had solid skills in key areas, just not the necessary ones for the broad management role he needed filled. The prospect of firing Dana filled Kevin with angst. She was well liked inside the company and had significant industry contacts. For personal and professional reasons, he wanted her to leave on positive terms, and with a soft landing. He knew she couldn't keep taking a high salary in his company, yet he didn't know how to encourage her to move on and couldn't imagine walking her to the door. He was stuck.

We took a walk around the virtuous circle of empathy. Our first stop: understanding. When Kevin thought about Dana outside of his firm, he realized that she was someone who was highly motivated by status and by maintaining a large circle of relationships. She had also shown signs of interest in entrepreneurship, although he had never explored that topic with her. When he began to see a path toward a win-win situation, he prepared for a big conversation with Dana.

When they talked, Kevin acknowledged how she must be feeling, knowing she was not as successful as she wanted to be. He related it to his last job before he started his firm, and how that encouraged him to chart his own course. They listened to each other and spoke unguardedly for two hours. At the end, Dana decided to try to start her own consulting practice with Kevin as her first client. He was happy to oblige.

Example 2: Empathy Creating Hope

While the last example was about empathic leadership on an individual basis, consider the broader-scale case of Fannie Mae. If you have a home mortgage, there's a good chance that Fannie Mae had a hand in it as a guarantor. For much of its history, Washington, D.C.-based Fannie Mae, with its skyrocketing stock prices and progressive work policies, has been viewed as a model company and a destination workplace.

That all changed abruptly in 2008 when Fannie Mae suddenly became synonymous with the housing crisis and found itself in the thick of a media and political storm. As part of the government's efforts to stabilize the financial sector, Fannie Mae was placed under conservatorship. Instead of the company's leadership deciding Fannie's future, Congress would.

Fannie Mae employees were morally devastated by what had

happened. The whole country seemed to be blaming them for the housing market collapse. Every day it seemed the media was conjuring up a new negative spin on Fannie Mae. Personal net worths and retirement savings plummeted with Fannie Mae's stock prices. Employees went from workplace pride to workplace embarrassment. And worst of all, no one knew what Congress planned to do with the company after the new Obama administration stepped in. People feared for their livelihoods and their futures.[8]

In September 2008, Herb Allison was appointed by Fannie Mae's conservator to step in as the CEO. During his tenure, Allison was a model of what empathic leadership could do. First and foremost, he was a communicator. He made sure everyone across the company—in all locations—knew what the corporate values were. He modeled brave leadership by making tough decisions and taking accountability. He spoke frankly about what he could control and what was out of his hands. He held weekly town hall–style videoconferences where any person could ask any question and he would answer it. People were scared, frustrated, and angry. But having the opportunity to take a question straight to the top *every week* spoke volumes. Allison showed Fannie's employees that he knew what they were going through, and that he would go to bat for them and the company. He was inspiring because he reached out, understood, and connected. He had authentic presence. (He was so effective that after only a few months President Obama tapped him to run the Treasury Department's Troubled Asset Relief Program, or TARP, created to buttress the nation's financial services industry.)

During this period, you could hear employees from the VP level to the custodial staff commenting that they felt Allison was looking out for them. People who had never laid eyes on him came to work every day feeling that they knew him.

Chris Segall, then director of talent management at Fannie Mae, put it this way: "When Herb spoke, you could hear a pin drop in the room. He projected wisdom, sincerity, and a firm conviction of what was right versus wrong. His capacity for listening to others was equally impressive. Regardless of your level in the company, you had his full attention. He listened as though each word you said mattered and might just contain the next revolutionary idea."[9]

Herb Allison's leadership was a bright light in an otherwise very tough time. He created hope.

It's a Circle for a Reason

Each time you go around a virtuous circle it gets easier. If you seek to understand, listen, acknowledge, and relate, then you'll ask better questions, strengthen your connections, and gain a deeper understanding of the situation.

Empathy creates better relationships and more successful outcomes. If there is a relationship that's weakened, empathy can build more intimacy and enhance overall trust. Think about what's holding you back. Then, if necessary, take a step out of your comfort zone.

Empathy that stays in your head unexpressed has zero effect.

Here's the big point for leaders: It's not enough just to have empathy; you have to show it. We all have empathic thoughts, but just like any killer app, if the idea stays in your head, the world remains unchanged.

Key Takeaways from Chapter 7

1. Most executives have been conditioned to aspire to an empathic leadership style. The breakdown is between knowing and doing.
2. Leaders often cite lack of time, personal discomfort, short-term goals, or a past incident as reasons they fail to get inside the heads of their team members.
3. There are multiple styles in empathic leadership. The stereotype of the group hugger is not the norm. Find a way to apply your authentic self in an empathic way.
4. Become a commonality-seeking machine. Look for authentic connections continuously in your interactions.
5. Creating empathy is a virtuous circle. When you are searching in the moment to truly identify with someone, remember to understand, listen, acknowledge, and relate.
6. It's not enough to feel empathy—you have to express it. If a tree falls in the forest . . . you know the rest.

Ideas I Want to Try from Chapter 7:

_____

_____

_____

_____

_____

CHAPTER 8

A Note to Emailphiles, Smartphone Addicts, and TurboTexters

Perhaps the title of this chapter makes you feel slightly defensive. Or maybe it makes you want to shout a resounding "Yes! Stop those people!" If you had either of those reactions—or if you are a living, breathing member of today's workforce—this chapter is for you.

I don't attempt to hide my bias toward face-to-face communication. Scads of research (besides Dr. Albert Mehrabian's, as discussed in Chapter 2) attest to the fact that we take one another in through multiple senses. When you eliminate most of them, there's bound to be misunderstanding.

Let's use Internet dating as an example. You can have a lovely exchange with someone through email in which you find the person to be witty, kind, and smart. Then you move to a phone conversation and get a fuller picture from verbal cues. But you don't really know someone until you meet in person. That's when the relationship begins (or, according to my single friends, when most online matches end).

The same is true at work. Ever meet someone whom you've only spoken with over the phone? Usually, our mental image of the person differs quite a bit from the actual human in front of us. When you

129

first meet, you have a moment of cognitive dissonance before reestablishing your perception of the person by taking in all of this new data.

Presence is a full-contact sport. With each layer of information we understand more of the other person. Writing gives us baseline information, verbal intonation a layer more, and finally body language provides a giant leap in understanding. That's why nuanced messages are communicated far more effectively in person.

> *Nuanced messages are communicated far more effectively in person.*

What does this mean for a society where email has become such a default communications vehicle that, without even thinking about it, we'll type to someone in an office next door? What does it mean when texting is replacing voice as the most used application on mobile phones? These days, leaving a voice message is beginning to feel quaint.

Please don't get the impression that I fail to appreciate people's love of electronic communications. I really, really do! While I wouldn't say I'm an early adopter, I'm definitely in the next wave. I love my smartphone, email prodigiously, blog, tweet, and text frequently. That said, I also see a lot of problems occurring because of overuse of these technologies. New norms are developing quickly, but not universally. Generational gaps are dividing companies. And there's a ton of bad behavior happening behind innocent-looking keyboards.

Now I know this book is about authentic executive presence and finding what feels right to you. I have tried to be more descriptive than prescriptive, and I will continue to do so—except in this chapter. I would be remiss if I wrote a book on presence and didn't include one of the most common derailers of presence: misuse of electronic communications. It comes up continually in companies. In fact, I bet you can spot yourself, or some of your colleagues, in the scenarios I'm about to describe.

So pardon my preachiness. And please avoid the following behaviors.

Scenario 1: Management by Email

You know you are managing via email when most of your directives, accolades, and communications happen through keystrokes. And there are many of you out there. Email is an effective management tool in many ways. The problem is that overreliance on it is decidedly ineffective—and not always for the reasons you may imagine. Take the quiz titled "Test Your Email Acumen" (located in the sidebar), and then read on to learn what works and what doesn't.

> *Email is an effective management tool. Overuse of email is decidedly not.*

||||||||||||||||||||||||||||||||||||||||||||||||||||||||||||||||||||||||||||||||||||||||||||

Test Your Email Acumen

Answer these three questions. Circle one or more answers that apply.

1. Using email for assigning projects usually:
   A. Saves time
   B. Wastes time
2. When a subordinate receives a work assignment from his supervisor via email that is unclear, he's most likely to:
   A. Ask for clarification
   B. Spend time conferring with others to get their take on the assignment
   C. Take a guess and do what he thinks
3. It's effective for a manager to use email to deliver:
   A. Good news (e.g., promotions, pats on the back, awards)
   B. Neutral news (e.g., process-related or administrative updates or reminders)
   C. Bad news (e.g., reprimands, constructive feedback)

||||||||||||||||||||||||||||||||||||||||||||||||||||||||||||||||||||||||||||||||||||||||||||

Managers know that they need to be in front of their teams to deliver their vision, rally the troops, and tackle uncertainty—in other words, the big stuff. But email tends to be a convenient default in the day-to-day realm of getting work done. Most managers will say that they use email in the interest of saving time. It's easier to delegate projects through email than by catching people on the phone or in their office between meetings. I would argue it's not generally the case that email is a time-saver. *The answer to question 1 is B.*

When assigning work, the most important aspect is to be clear about your expectations. This generally requires a give-and-take about content, resources, and deadlines. If that process is absent, you are likely to run into a lot of time-consuming inefficiencies.

When projects are understood and underway, email can be enormously efficient at managing a group of people toward a final delivery. However, depending on the complexity, you may still need verbal check-ins. That leads us to the question of what subordinates do when they receive unclear work assignments via email. *The answer to question 2 is both B and C.*

The primary reason email wastes time is that guesswork is involved when a directive isn't fully understood. Perhaps it's a human response to authority, but we don't like to burden our boss with a lot of follow-up conversation in response to an email. Email has a way of creating distance. When a manager sends messages via email, the impression is that she might not want to be interrupted by in-person conversation, whether or not it's true (and let's be honest, sometimes it is true).

More than likely, we'll go elsewhere for the answer, which of course only increases the likelihood that we're off base. When I learn that an executive is not getting back the quality of work that he expects, I'll ask him to describe his delegation process. Typically, it starts with an email.

There are also times when email works well. *The answer to question 3 is A and B.*

Using email to rev up the whole team behind recent wins or to highlight corporate events allows everyone to be "in the know" simultaneously. Calling out an employee for excellent performance, either in a group email or individually, can be gratifying. It allows the employee to read the positive review multiple times, send it to friends and family, and get pats on the back all day from his coworkers.

> Use email for positive or neutral communications—never for the negative.

And you can't beat email for outlining neutral information such as administrative processes that require detailed explanation or reminders. Clearly, a push to submit better expense reports doesn't warrant a staff meeting. Thank you, Microsoft Outlook, for saving us from those sonorous meetings.

Now here's where email should never be used: to communicate bad news. And I would even add, anything that could be *interpreted* as bad news. First of all, for the recipient, getting a negative email feels rotten. You're missing valuable context. You can't ask questions or present your side. It shreds your productivity. When you get such an email, you don't read it and get back to work. You stew on it. Send it to your spouse. Update your resume. In the absence of important cues from the sender that would make the communications productive, there's usually nothing to act on. If the manager's goal is to correct behavior or direct attention to a problem, a negative email accomplishes very little of that.

One last note: Employees frequently complain about the volume of emails from their managers. It's not that they don't expect emails. It's simply that they want to get some work done in between reading so many emails. Check your sent box and see if you are emailing the same people more than three times per day. If you are, then you may be managing by email. Try to consolidate your correspondence so that your team feels less barraged. Or try an old trick: Just get up and walk down the hall.

Scenario 2: The Never-Ending Workday of 24/7 Emails

I regularly hear complaints that someone's manager (including the CEO) constantly emails. It's not simply the volume that's distressing; it's the lack of boundaries. The emails don't just come during the workday, but at 6 a.m. or midnight or on Sunday at 2 p.m. It creates the impression that work is never over, and that the employee must always be on the job. Employees then drop everything and rush to respond to keep up the pace. Here's the interesting part: Managers will often say that they email when an idea hits them, not necessarily because they expect the employee to respond. However, there's a power dynamic at play. The leader sets the tone. And when the boss's emails don't respect boundaries, the inference is that there aren't any.

By the way, constantly emailing can damage a manager's reputation. It makes him appear scattered, inefficient, one-dimensional, or sorely lacking in time management skills. We want our leaders to work hard, but we also want them to have a life.

Constant emailing is mainly an issue for the manager to address. If you want your team to be burned out and resentful, 24/7 emails are the way to go. Otherwise, give people the courtesy of having a life. And if you are on the receiving end, holding off on your response until the normal workday (assuming it's not truly urgent) or waiting 24 hours on the weekend is perfectly acceptable and gently establishes boundaries.

> *If you want your team to feel burned out and resentful, burden them with constant emails.*

Scenario 3: You've Got a Nastygram

Nastygrams go beyond bad news. These are sent with malicious intent and vitriol. They are the equivalent of a sucker punch by someone who is too much of a coward to say something to your face. You see this firsthand if you've ever confronted someone who has sent a nastygram. The backpedaling starts immediately.

The genesis of a nastygram is usually something like this: Someone gets angry, either by a personal affront or work gone wrong. And the sender pours all that anger out in a cathartic email. And hits the Send button. (These are often worse late in the day.)

Nearly everyone has sent one nasty email at some point. Some people get a reputation for sending them. When you see their name pop up in your inbox, you get a pit in your stomach.

Whatever the circumstances, there's a simple trick for whenever you find yourself furiously typing away on an emotional missive: Save a draft and sleep on it. This eliminates 99 percent of the issue because after the anger subsides, the same email will rarely go out. Sending emails in anger doesn't accomplish anything; in fact, it ruins connection (once bitten, twice shy) and can even get you fired.

> *When in doubt if your email is appropriate, save a draft and sleep on it.*

As a leader, practice common courtesy when sending email. With the power dynamic thrown in, even sparsely worded emails can seem to have a tone of frustration. Again, when there are no cues to be drawn from the sender's personal presence, the email's recipients are left hanging on the small lines and curves on their screens.

Scenario 4: Hostile Reply-Alls

This scenario combines a few of the previous points. Most of us have seen someone on an email thread suddenly call out another person on the thread through a "reply all" message. It's essentially the same as being dressed down in a meeting. It can get worse, such as when the recipient tries to discuss the issue privately, only to have the other person reply by bringing the full group back on the email! It's downright hostile behavior.

I had a client whose manager hit the Reply-all button so frequently that he refused to respond to emails. It created an environment of fear and retaliation. He tried to address it directly with his manager but was never successful. No surprise that he moved on.

Suffice it to say that this strategy accomplishes little. Whether it's a group of peers or colleagues at mixed levels, as soon as any individual's issue turns the least bit negative, get off the group email and handle it one-on-one. If it seems like it could be embarrassing to discuss in a group, it is.

Scenario 5: Paging Dr. Smartphone

Not only is "smartphone addiction" one of my pet peeves, but it's a definite presence detractor as well. We cling to our smartphones as if we are all doctors being paged to perform life-saving surgery. Nearly every meeting has people who constantly check their devices for new messages. You sit at lunch with someone whose phone sits right at the table, faceup, to check on a whim. Why do people who aren't even in the room take precedent over someone who makes the effort to be right in front of us?

It's ridiculous, but we seldom recognize the ridiculousness of the situation. Instead, we experience it as rudeness, plain and simple. If you behave this way, you are sending a not-so-subtle message that those you are with are *less than* someone else. Less important. Less critical. Less interesting. Less deserving of your time.

If you are trying to strengthen your presence, you won't get there by making those around you feel diminished.

Staying glued to your mobile device diminishes others and makes you look like a lackey.

I know successful executives who, despite their busy lives, are artful at checking their smartphones in private. Their companies survive—and thrive—without them constantly checking their mobile devices. So, don't be a lackey to yours.

Scenario 6: Unintentional Social Media Notoriety

I'm of two minds about social media in the workplace. Here are the positives: Facebook, Twitter, and to a certain extent LinkedIn (and all the similar sites coming out every day) have put a human face on coworkers. We can learn more about people by scanning their Facebook page than working with them for a year. (Who knew Dave in legal played guitar?) It encourages us to show our authentic, unvarnished selves in their totality. In fact, social media norms dictate that you should be informal and personal, lest you risk standing out as gauche or "sales-y." Most executives I know blend respectable personal details with a bit of information about their work. They show a witty or introspective side that doesn't always come out in the office. It's a good thing.

Here comes the *but*. . . .

I also see people making corporate faux pas with social media technology. There are the big examples, such as the spate of journalists who have been fired or reprimanded for using Twitter in a way that was deemed inappropriate. Mostly though, we are exposed to small discomforts that make us squirm in our seats when we read them. Consider when professional colleagues:

— Use social media to share polarizing political or religious positions.

— Post and share racy or suggestive photos.

— Discuss corporate information that isn't confidential, but shouldn't be shared, either.

— Get tagged on an old friend's site in photos that are not ready for prime time.

— Use social media sites as essentially an email list to spam the entire group about events and personal updates.

— Update their network or tweet too frequently, in effect presenting an image of someone who has too much time on his hands.

— Maintain a controversial or discordant blogger or Twitter persona.

These are a few common examples. You can undoubtedly add more to the list. If you are using social media to enhance your presence and build connection, you need to make sure your efforts don't create barriers. You certainly don't want to alienate people. Ask yourself, do your social media communications support your intention?

We're all still trying to reconcile how to use these sites. A few years ago, communicating to friends and coworkers in one information stream would have seemed crazy. We're getting better about differentiating what's appropriate and what's not. Updates to Facebook and the rollout of Google+ offer new options for grouping contacts. As a general rule, though, I advise you to post to Facebook or Twitter the way you would speak in person to a mixed work group over lunch. If you wouldn't say it there, don't put it on social media. Some people choose to operate two different sites for work and home. Just remember, it's hard to hide online.

Is Disintermediation Coming Back in Style?

There is some hope that perhaps this intermediation through electronics isn't solving the world's problems after all. Just as societies typically swing far to the extreme before coming back to a sustainable middle ground, companies have begun to realize the inherent problems of social networks and are developing guidelines similar to policies they already have around email use. Businesses are actively finding ways to bridge global and spatial divides. It's exciting to witness and experience these technology breakthroughs that make connection easier and more personal.

I can't wait to see what happens next. In the meantime, I'll be keeping my smartphone under the table and my political opinions off Facebook.

Key Takeaways from Chapter 8

1. Electronic mail communications often have a deleterious effect on presence. Our perceptions of others are predicated on multiple senses and with only writing to go on, misunderstandings are commonplace.

2. Managers set the tone for email use in companies. Be aware of both the volume and the content of your emails. If effective delegation is a problem, email is a likely culprit.
3. As a general rule, use email for positive and neutral information. For negative content, deliver the bad news in person. Phone is second best.
4. Checking mobile devices in the company of others is a definite presence detractor. It diminishes the person in front of you. This seems obvious, and yet the practice is rampant.
5. Social media has to support your personal presence intention. Realize that it's one more data point that people use to understand you, and it is most effective when it combines selective, appropriate personal information with your professional life.

Ideas I Want to Try from Chapter 8:

_____

_____

_____

_____

_____

PART 3

INSPIRATIONAL

Communicating to Build and Motivate Followership

CHAPTER 9

Inspiring Change
from the Brain Down

The final pillar of I-Presence is about being *inspirational*—using our presence to influence others. It's the quality most people generally associate with executive presence, though now you know there's a whole backstory as well. In the Introduction, when I established the I-Presence model, I talked about inner presence and outer presence. Part 1 focused on our deepest inner presence and being *intentional,* while Part 2 married our *individual* thoughts and actions to those of others in order to form authentic connections. Next, we'll ensconce ourselves squarely in the realm of our outer game.

This final part on inspiring other people clarifies and integrates many of the ideas presented in the first two parts of the book. I'll take a practical approach to help you build influence and followership so that the concepts are manageable. Some of the tools presented will be familiar, but with a new twist; others may be well outside your comfort zone. That's to be expected. To be inspiring, you must exhibit your full presence; you have to stand out and get noticed. So at times, you'll be stretching.

Being inspirational means that you are a change agent. As corporate hierarchies have flattened and the demand for creative, conceptual work has risen, old models of communicating no longer work so well. You cannot say, "Do this because I'm your boss and I say so," and expect other people to automatically act or think differently. We need our teams and coworkers to take our ideas, internalize solutions, and personally buy into them. We want to invite them to our way of thinking, not grab them by the neck to get there.

When you inspire others, you are altering their thoughts, perspectives, or actions. They are different as a result of your exchange. Yep, you are in the change business. And while you may have heard the saying that the only constant in life is change, I'd add that the only constant about change is that it's hard.

Inspiring requires change. Leaders are change agents.

If we can't understand, embrace, and precipitate change, we'll never inspire others. So that's where we are going to begin. Before we jump into discussing the tools you can use to inspire others, it's helpful to understand what holds back change and what encourages it on the deepest levels.

Change Starts with You

When it comes to inspiring change, there are two audiences you need to consider: yourself and everyone else. First, think about how to change yourself (that's why you are reading this book). If you never act on any of the ideas presented here, this will be one more business book you read and then put on the shelf (and neither one of us wants that to happen). It's one thing to find new concepts interesting and quite another to take consistent action and make sustained changes. This first step of embracing and managing change in yourself is critical and, at times, the hardest to undertake.

First learn to change yourself. Then you'll know how to change everyone else.

Second, consider how your ideas create change in others. What makes people either readily accept or flat-out reject your message? There are universal human responses to change. Understanding them enables you to frame your own communications to be heard with optimal clarity.

Here's the easy part: Turns out that what makes it difficult for you to change is the same thing that makes it difficult for your audience to change. No one is trying to be intractable.

You can blame it on the brain.

It's Not My Fault, My Brain Made Me Do It!
(Neuroscience, the Abridged Version)

In the past decade, neuroscience has exploded with findings about how our brain manages information and forms decisions. Using advanced functional MRI (fMRI) technology to scan the brain in the midst of cognitive processes, scientists can now observe and measure neural activity inside the brain as we perform our daily functions. What was once intuitive is now scientifically verifiable.

Neuroscience research is having an impact on nearly every segment of medicine, psychology, and the social sciences. It's creating new fields such as neuromarketing and neuroeconomics. Management is on the cusp of a neuroscience tidal wave, too. Go on any popular newsmagazine's website and type in "neuroscience." You'll find articles written about its application to leadership and business. Brain science in the boardroom is approaching mainstream.

I was first exposed to neuroscience research in the late 1990s as a lay reader. Subsequently, as someone who makes a living by influencing human behavior, I've kept an interest in it. Clearly, I'm not a neuroscientist, and I suspect most of you reading this book aren't, either. Slogging through the scholarly articles and scientific research findings on neurotransmitters and synapses can be mind-numbing. If you are looking for practical business implications, it's tough going. But we shouldn't ignore the findings about how people create change and form decisions. The research has deep implications for inspirational leadership.

For this chapter, I'm condensing a wide swath of neuroscience research into definable points that are relevant to our discussion of presence. (If you are interested in reading more, I've included references throughout the chapter and in the notes section to some of my favorite books on the subject.) To help put these top-line thoughts together, I interviewed David Rock, one of the pioneers in a new field that he has coined *neuroleadership*. As you may guess, neuroleadership combines neuroscience with leadership. Rock is a prolific writer on the topic, including recent books *Quiet Leadership* and *Your Brain at Work*.[1] Rock has also developed a think tank of sorts—the Neuroleadership Institute—which is made up of an interdisciplinary group of scholars and practitioners.

Rock does the herculean job of condensing tomes of research into practical business implications (for *Your Brain at Work* he interviewed 30 neuroscientists). Considering the relevance of Rock's work, it's no surprise that he is in demand as a speaker and a consultant to companies that are trying to create change or improve performance. Here are some of the neuroleadership findings that are generating "*Aha!* moments" in corporations around the globe— and have enormous relevance to your presence objectives.

Your Brain Prefers Life in a Worn, Comfortable Recliner

From our earliest stages of development, we begin constructing mental maps of the world around us. The maps we create become actual neural circuits—connections between distinct neurons. These connections form thoughts. As neuroscientists put it, what fires together gets wired together.

These mental maps create our automatic responses: Touching something hot means we'll get burned. Our mental maps also create our most intricate thoughts about the world. Everyone's maps are unique and distinctly designed based on an individual's particular life experiences. Even when the conclusion is the same as nearly everyone else's, the mental maps we've created to get there are ours alone. We may all think the United States is a great country, but how we build that belief is based on our individual perceptions.

In the brain, what fires together gets wired together.

When we are in the analyzing phase of a thought, we keep it in our prefrontal cortex, which is responsible for executive brain functioning. This is where our short-term memory resides and our heaviest mental lifting happens. The prefrontal cortex has very limited horsepower compared to the rest of our brain, and it requires an inordinate amount of energy. This explains why complex thinking wears us out, and why it's been proven repeatedly that true multitasking is a myth (what we call "multitasking" is actually just alternating from one task to another, and generally being less effective at everything). As we consider new thoughts in our prefrontal cortex, we are constantly accessing and comparing them against our mental maps, which are already formed and reside across various other parts of the brain. For example, if we have an enjoyable vacation in Colorado, we compare it to our existing maps about our last trip to Arizona, and the one five years ago to Maine, and what we read yesterday about the rising cost of family travel.

Our brain has evolved to be as energy efficient as possible. We can't hold many thoughts in our prefrontal cortex for long, so they are either forgotten or else they get hardwired to our long-term memory. At that point, thoughts are embedded in lower-energy storage as trillions of neural connections throughout the brain composed of visual, auditory, and other senses that are consolidated to create long-term memory. The brain is adept at lighting up these connections when it needs them, especially for the maps that have gotten a lot of attention. It requires little energy (or conscious thought) to sing a song you know well, but learning to sing an Italian opera would be outright taxing for most of us. We'd need to concentrate fully to have a chance of even remembering the words, let alone singing them (and afterward, we'd be exhausted, ready to veg out in front of the TV or take a nap).

The brain strives for efficiency. Therefore, reinforcing our current mental maps, which are essentially our thoughts and perceptions, feels good to us. When we see information that confirms our existing perceptions, the grooves between point A and point B on our maps become better established. Energy is saved. When we see data that disproves our existing perceptions, our thoughts spend more time in our prefrontal cortex as we compare and contrast against existing mental maps. Loads more energy gets used.

Think of the importance of this finding as it relates to change: Our brain is built to resist change because doing so enhances efficiency and saves energy. We are optimized to seek out information that confirms what we already believe to be true, and to avoid information that goes against our existing belief system.

This is critical information to have

Our brains achieve energy efficiency by confirming what we already believe. It feels best to us.

about yourself as you encounter new ideas (such as those you are discovering in this book). It's absolutely natural, from our deepest biology, to resist change and new ideas. However, there exists a sort of social folklore that we should rely on our first instincts to decide what's good or bad for us. If we have a gut feeling to avoid something, then we should because it's not right for us. I simply want to offer another explanation: Perhaps your initial reaction isn't actually instinctual foresight, but your brain's automatic response to a dissonant idea. We crave the familiar, the comfortable, and the path of least resistance. Anything else is going to set off some alarms.

"We have a lot of automatic response to the world," says Rock. "Most of our responses are automatic and unconscious. Our brains prefer certainty to uncertainty. Certainty activates a reward response, while uncertainty activates our threat circuits. A small level of uncertainty is a novelty, but anything above a small level of uncertainty quickly feels like pain."

And Yet You Don't Have to Watch a Midlife Crisis to Know People Change Every Day

Now, you may wonder: How does anyone ever learn and grow? But of course we know that personal development is an integral part of being human and can be a great joy in life. We confront new ideas all the time. The brain is constantly changing, taking in fresh information, forming new mental maps, and adapting old ones. The brain's malleability, or *neuroplasticity,* is nothing short of awe-inspiring. Think of how your thoughts differ today from when you were 15 years old, or even last year. We are all profoundly glad we don't walk around with the same brain our whole lives.

So how do we change our thoughts, and their ensuing behaviors, most effectively? We know that it's hard work to change an ingrained perception that requires rewiring an existing mental map. As it turns out, it's much easier to create entirely new mental maps. And on top of it, we even get an energy boost.

It's far easier to create new mental maps than to change existing ones.

Consider this familiar scenario: You go to hear a compelling speaker, perhaps in a training or workshop setting. As the speaker talks, you may have an impulse to sit back for a second to ponder, which means you are comparing this new data against your existing mental maps. You analyze how the new ideas fit in with what you've observed. And then, in a burst of energy, you think, *Aha!* You get excited about this fresh idea. Suddenly some pieces come together and you are ready to take action or share what you've learned. You've just created a new mental map! Even better, that burst of energy you felt was adrenaline being released, which gives you a lift. (You can actually observe this response in someone, and it doesn't take state-of-the-art brain scanning equipment. It's all over a person's face.)

You leave the training excited to go out and apply your new learning. Then you return to your office and begin going through all the emails that have collected, and before you know it you're thrown into a minor crisis. In other words, essentially, life takes over. Does this story sound familiar? A few days after the training you struggle to remember what you were so excited about earlier in the week. When you try to explain it to a colleague, you find yourself straining to recall how all the details fit together. The moment has passed, and you've lost the motivation to take action on your new insight.

Insights are energizing but fleeting.

What I've just described happens to all of us. When I was a CEO member of Vistage International, we had engaging speakers come in every month speaking on topics such as revamping sales and marketing, HR processes, and leadership models. It was a well-worn joke among our staffs that when we returned to our offices afterward, fresh with new insights, our teams would roll their eyes and think, "Good grief, here she goes again!" They knew to wait it out, because our enthusiasm for overhauling the status quo would fade within a week or so. Some ideas stuck, but most never made it to action.

Five Steps to Optimize Your Brain for Change

So where does that leave someone who wants to turn insights into action? We know that creating a new mental map is key. But the way to keep it alive is through focused attention. Rock explains the power of attention this way: "Like most things, it's a whole brain phenomenon. Attention is like an entire orchestra coming to a note. When we're not paying attention, our brain is like an orchestra all playing at once. When we pay attention, it all becomes synchronized and the circuits start firing together, which helps to create long-term memories."

Rock is referring to "attention density" (a term coined by Dr. Jeffrey Schwartz). To sustain a new mental map—to wear the newly established grooves down so that they become a default path—we have to keep the focus on what we are trying to accomplish with frequency, intensity, and deliberation. For most of us, that means being purposeful about setting up processes and systems to make change happen. If you want to create lasting behavior change around the presence ideas in this book (or anything else you care about), here are some helpful steps.

Step 1: Make Room for Reflection Time

Intuitively, we know that it's important to have a chance to look inward and gather our thoughts and collect ourselves. In leadership coaching, it's a nearly universal strategy to help clients improve their effectiveness by building in reflection time (other names for it are "strategic thinking," "planning time," or "prioritization"). The brain benefits from contemplation in specific ways. As Rock puts it, when we aren't focusing, our neural circuits are lighting up in a cacophony of thoughts. Being reflective quiets the mind; it allows us to observe our own thoughts as we process connections and access mental maps.

Being reflective involves taking a cerebral step back. It's not about forcing our full mental heft on the problem at hand. It's about creating space to allow thoughts to come to us (and old mental maps to be dug out of our gray matter). In his book about human motivation, *Drive,* Daniel Pink talks about the phenomenon of functional fixedness.[2] It's the scientifically validated idea that when we are overly focused on the most obvious definition or use of something, we can't see alternative definitions or uses. Researchers have created puzzles to illustrate functional fixedness. You've likely seen such puzzles where, for instance, objects such as boxes must be turned into trays in order to meet the objective, but people can't see past the use of the boxes as containers. Another example is where subjects are presented with a familiar sentence that has alternative meanings, yet all but the most obvious one escapes them. This concept has been proved in studies across cultures, decades, and ages. All people over the age of seven have some degree of functional fixedness at work in their brains.

Now, let's put it all together: The human brain's propensity to validate what we already believe, and to get fixated on the most obvious answer, handicaps our capacity for creativity, expansive ideation, and unfamiliar men-

Reflection time involves letting thoughts come to us, which helps overcome functional fixedness.

tal shifts. When we purposefully quiet the loud parts of our minds and create room for emergent ideas, then we are more likely to process those ideas fully and build the all-important neural pathways that create insights.

Your Brain and Presence: Action Item 1

Find a quiet place in your office or home. Once there, think about the ideas in this book that felt right to you. Also, which ideas created an automatic discomfort? How would you like to approach your presence going forward?

You may find it helpful to write down your thoughts, make a list of ideas to try, or draw a diagram of your plan going forward. Or simply turn off all distractions and just think.

Step 2: Focus on Solutions, Not Problems

Attention shapes our mental maps. By pivoting our attention we can begin to develop new modes of thinking and doing. Consider your brain to be like a muscle: The thoughts we work on the most get stronger. If we keep our attention on what's wrong or on our failures, those thoughts will dominate our minds. Alternatively, if we choose to focus on what's working or what's possible, those thoughts become more vivid. That's why focusing on problems over solutions can hold us back on every level.

Unfortunately, our societal culture often encourages us to remain in the problem phase. We are rewarded for getting to the bottom of what's wrong in a situation. When circumstances go awry at work, we spend hours in meetings discussing what happened. When an employee messes up, we bring her in our office to understand how she failed. As I wrote about in Chapter 3, most psychological treatment requires involved discussions of negative emotions and personal limitations (which has spawned Martin Seligman's groundbreaking work in positive psychology, as well as a groundswell of antidepressant drugs). The tendency is to go to the problem phase quickly—and usually lull there. When we do that, our negative mental maps are pumping iron.

When we focus on problems, our negative mental maps are pumping iron.

When we are trying to create change, we have a far better chance of succeeding if we make a concerted effort to focus on solutions. (Of course we need to understand the basics of the problem, so we don't repeat it, but beyond that, the future is in the solution.) This goes for us personally as well as professionally. If we focus on our weaknesses, then we buy into our limitations. If we spend our mental energy on our strengths, we see our potential. In coaching, we use a technique called *appreciative inquiry* to foster and strengthen new positive mental maps. Through a series of questions, we guide clients to what's right and possible and pull them out of the morass of what's wrong.

As you encounter ideas in this book, your first response might be, "I'm not good at communicating because I'm an introvert" or "Whenever I speak to a group I get nervous." Keep your focus there and it will continue to be true. But if you want to inspire yourself to change, recognize resistance as a natural default, based on your existing mental maps, and try to lasso your thoughts. Don't buy into the cultural norm of focusing on the problem. Consider solutions instead. To extend the example, your perceived introversion can make you a keen observer of others, which is a critical skill in executive presence. Perhaps you can reframe your thoughts around nervousness to consider that while you have felt anxious in the past, with practice and repetition you'll gain confidence the next time you have to speak before a group. (Plus, you learned how to abate your nervousness using the tools in Chapter 3.)

||||||||||||||||||||||||||||||||||||||||||||||||||||||||||||||||||||||||||||||||||||||||||||||||

Your Brain and Presence: Action Item 2

As you try out the ideas in the book, take note of where your mind naturally goes. Are you quick to determine why something won't work? To break this habit, try for an 80/20 rule. Spend 80 percent of your thought time on solutions, and only 20 percent on the problem.

Two questions to ask yourself:

- What strengths do I bring to this presence concept?
- What would success with this concept look like for me?

||||||||||||||||||||||||||||||||||||||||||||||||||||||||||||||||||||||||||||||||||||||||||||||||

Step 3: Strike While the *Aha!* Moments Are Hot

It feels great when we get that release of adrenaline from newly formed connections. We are primed to take action in that moment, but the clock is ticking on our excitement. You'll have far greater success with change if you can capture that moment and act quickly, or at least create a path to action.

The easiest action to take is to write down your ideas. Sketch out your thoughts *in the moment,* so you can recall them when the adrenaline rush is over and your brain is flooded with other thoughts. (Use the "Ideas I Want to Try" sections at the end of each chapter to capture new insights.) It can also be helpful to set a clear personal goal for yourself that will keep you on track and bring the new idea or behavior into the reality of your daily life.

One of the elements of attention density is frequency, or ensuring that you revisit desired behavioral change again and again. Rock adds, "If you want to sustain change, you need to set up your environment to keep that change alive. That means having reminders in the forms of systems, processes and people."

Having a personal executive coach to hold you accountable is a huge benefit, but not one that's within reach for most people. Finding a colleague who can keep you to task and provide feedback also works. Top executive coach and author Marshall Goldsmith coined the term *feed forward,* a process whereby you let colleagues know ahead of time what you are working on so they can share what they observe in natural occurrences.[3]

Finally, stating our intended change in public creates intrinsic motivation to achieve it. A technique I've used is to go around the room after a meeting and have people state what they are committing to. Those things we promise out loud and in front of others are more likely to get done; so let others know what you're up to.

If you want to keep an insight active, sketch it out, revisit it often, become accountable for it, and broadcast it.

In short, the next time you want to turn an insight into an action, sketch it out, revisit it often, become accountable for it, and broadcast it.

||||||||||||||||||||||||||||||||||||||||||||||||||||||||||||||||||||||||||||||||||||||||||||||||||||||||

Your Brain and Presence: Action Item 3

Go back through the previous chapters and reread what you filled out in the "Ideas I Want to Try" sections. If you haven't filled them out, start doing so from this chapter forward.

Select one tool or idea you want to put into practice. Sketch out how you can apply it, with as much detail as possible, including actual scenarios. Or tell a trusted colleague and have him observe you at work and provide feedback.

||||||||||||||||||||||||||||||||||||||||||||||||||||||||||||||||||||||||||||||||||||||||||||||||||||||||

Step 4: Just Do It (At Least in a Small Way)

The goal of many coaches is transformational change; that is, helping the client to make a significant mental shift that alters behavior. It's rewarding to be part of a profound positive change. Change can definitely happen that way, but it usually doesn't. Instead, people make incremental change, gain some confidence and perspective, and then try the next goal. It's much more comfortable for people to envision a tangible, discrete step than to jump to a faraway place they've never been before. Change is a process. If our brains sense some degree of certainty, then we are more likely to be open to change and allow it to happen. One of the themes of this book is to incorporate a few new behaviors that feel most comfortable and see what fits, then continue building from there. I wanted to avoid the mental shutdown that comes with uncertainty or the wholesale reorientation of a person's modus operandi.

As it turns out, there's also science behind Nike's famous slogan to "Just Do It." Taking that first step (just doing it), and seeing success, has a profound impact on the brain. A 2009 study led by neuroscientist Earl Miller at MIT's Picower Institute for Learning and Memory showed

The brain learns more from success than from failure.

that we absorb more lessons from success than from failure.[4] Furthermore, each ensuing success is processed more efficiently. Because the brain doesn't know exactly what to retain from most failures to safeguard against future failures, it doesn't exhibit the same type of neuroplasticity as it does with successes. We learn quickly what made us succeed.

Learning new ideas is rewarding, but if we want our thoughts and behaviors to truly change, we have to put ourselves out there—even if it's one step at a time. It's one more way that success breeds success.

Your Brain and Presence: Action Item 4

Take the step. Put into practice the idea that you wrote about in Action Item 3. If you can't do it today, put it on your calendar. Make a commitment to yourself!

Step 5: Find Your Flow

In his seminal work that created an eponymous business term, *Flow,* psychologist Mihaly Csikszentmihalyi laid out his research findings on what creates intrinsic joy in our work and in our lives.[5] Flow happens in those moments when we feel "in the zone," when we are immersed in an activity, lose track of time, and bring our full skills to bear. In *Drive,* Dan Pink brings flow into the conversation of how to create internal motivation in our age of conceptual, right-brained work. Pink discusses the need to create goals that are just enough of a stretch for people to seek mastery, but not too far out of their capability to cause frustration. This aligns with what David Rock has observed about a little uncertainty being a novelty.

We all sense flow in our own lives. If you think back to your most rewarding and exciting projects, there were likely moments of flow. You can create the same experience around your presence objectives. Start with incremental steps, trying new behaviors that are a small stretch. Set a goal for yourself that causes you to extend your capabilities or puts you on the path of mastery. The joy of flow is in the process.

> *Flow is when we feel in the zone and are bringing our full attention and skills to bear on an activity.*

||||||||||||||||||||||||||||||||||||||||||||||||||||||||||||||||||||||||||||||||||||||||||||||||||||||||

Your Brain and Presence: Action Item 5

Think about the behavior change you decided to make happen in Action Item 4. Now figure out your next one or two stretch steps. Remember, the idea is to keep improving—one manageable stretch at a time.

||||||||||||||||||||||||||||||||||||||||||||||||||||||||||||||||||||||||||||||||||||||||||||||||||||||||

Now That You're Inspired, It's Time to Inspire Others

Any of these suggestions about how to inspire yourself can be used to inspire others. You can see how readily focusing on solutions or enabling flow would work in managing people or teams. These suggestions may reinforce effective management practices that you already use. Now you know the science behind why they work!

At times, our need to inspire is less about initiating practices and more about the subtle art of influence. We need to communicate so that others hear us with clarity and take that personal leap to buy into our message. In those moments, our only tool is our full and total presence. We're transmitters hoping for clear and successful reception. Here are some ways to increase the odds.

Rock offers a compelling model for a mental environment that is conducive to influencing change. We've all heard of fight-or-flight, that reaction deep in our limbic systems that causes us to respond to external stimuli in an avoidant way. According to neuroscientists, fight-or-flight is a central organizing principle of the brain. We are constantly on alert to determine if anything, or anyone, will lead to a reward or a threat. This impacts our cognitive function in real ways. When our threat response is activated, oxygen and glucose are drawn from our prefrontal cortex (the working memory and higher-level, decision-making part of the brain). In that state, we lack the ability to perform at our most rational, cognitive best. What's more, we are limited from accessing the brain's full cognitive power. Consequently, we are likely to miss subtle cues needed for informed processing.

In our daily lives, we have a parallel interior world where we constantly assess others as either friend or foe. When we are in doubt—as with strangers or even those people we don't know well—our default is to assume that the other person is a foe. This has a remarkable implication for communication. Rock explains, "You don't process what a foe says using the same neural circuits as you use when processing what a friend says. If someone is a friend you process what they say using the same circuitry as you process your own thoughts. That's not the case when you think someone is a foe."

You can easily see how this fight-or-flight response can be beneficial from an evolutionary standpoint. If a tiger is chasing you, your best chance of survival is to shut out everything and run. However, humans are very complex animals; our limbic systems aren't activated only by physical threats. Stress can produce it, and stressors come in many forms.

> When we feel stressed or threatened, our cognitive functioning is limited.

Rock defines five social triggers that result in a threat-reward response. He calls the triggers "SCARF," which stands for status, certainty, autonomy, relatedness, and fairness (see Figure 9-1). The brain seeks to minimize threat in each of these five areas and maximize reward. If we can create an environment that keeps positive attention on the elements of SCARF, then we're more likely to influence and change behavior. Think of it as creating an optimal listening environment where your audience can tune in to what you are saying and tune out of the reactive mode. In other words, more thoughtful consideration and less thought about being chased by tigers.

S = Status
C = Certainty
A = Autonomy
R = Relatedness
F = Fairness

Figure 9-1. SCARF model.

SOURCE: From David Rock, *Your Brain at Work* (New York: Harper Business, 2009) p. 196.

Let's break down the elements of SCARF and discuss them further:

Status People feel rewarded when their status is protected or increased. Heightened status is the feeling of being more than something else, which could mean being smarter, wealthier, more successful, or higher up the hierarchical chain. Our status increases when we are publicly appreciated, promoted, or acknowledged for being smart and capable. Anything that makes someone feel less respected or appreciated can cause a status threat.

Certainty We are most at ease when we know what's going to happen next, and when the future fits with our existing perceptions. Certainty reduces cognitive dissonance. Of course, it's not always possible to know every next turn in business, but the more expectation setting you can do, and the more detail you can give about timelines, the less threatened others will feel.

Autonomy People like to think that they have control over their own fates and as much of their daily lives as possible. We enjoy the certainty of knowing what's expected, and we are least threatened when we aren't micromanaged about how to get there. Autonomy gives us a sense of personal agency (in neuroscience terms, the ability to originate and direct our own actions) that respects our individuality.

Relatedness All of us can recall a time when we felt the sting of social rejection. We feel threatened when we are excluded from social groups and rewarded when we are part of them. Thus, we form groups constantly because the sense of being one of the team is fulfilling, especially if you believe you are an important part of the team (status). Anyone who qualifies as a foe—whether a stranger, competitor, or saboteur—creates a threat response. This explains why finding commonalities and forging connections is critical for influencing.

Fairness   People want to be treated fairly. We are keenly frustrated when we sense a situation is unfair or unjust (consider how an undeserved promotion can wreak havoc on a corporate culture). The more that people can be assured that a decision is fair and balanced, the easier it will be for them to accept it.

The social triggers of SCARF are easy to understand because they hit home. Keeping them in mind when you need to persuade or motivate others will only help you communicate more clearly. Consider the next time you need to deliver a change message. Are you on the reward side or the threat side of SCARF? With a few message tweaks, you can achieve greater resonance, buy-in, and success.

The Human Drive to Connect to a Higher Purpose

For a good portion of my career I've worked with entrepreneurial technology companies. It's common to see people take lower wages, work longer hours, and put blood, sweat, and tears into a company that may or may not survive a year. For many people outside the industry, this seems crazy. How many times have we learned that you can't pay the mortgage with stock options and a promise? Why would people put themselves through this aggravation?

The answer is that entrepreneurial companies often create a strong sense of purpose for their employees. New technologies are changing industries, shaping the way we live, and leaving a legacy. (Imagine a world without Google or Facebook, or the PC for that matter.) For the people who work in technology start-ups, yes, there is a chance to get rich. Yet everyone but the most naive knows that's a gamble. What smart entrepreneurial companies guarantee is a chance to be part of something larger than any individual, and maybe even to be part of history.

You don't have to recall great philosophic debates on man's search for meaning to know that purpose is motivating. Humans crave it. Gallup Organization's well-known and exhaustively researched Q[12] engagement survey tests for purpose. Look at Barack Obama's 2008 purpose-driven presidential campaign. Whatever your politics or history's final judgment on Obama, it's a fact that he mobilized millions of people (many of whom had never voted before) to cast their ballots, including a historic number of younger voters, through use of exciting rhetoric about how to be part of change in America.

Purpose inspires people to self-motivate. Yet, in many companies and in our daily work lives, purpose can be hard to find. In *Drive,* Dan Pink says that providing a sense of purpose within organizations is a critical success factor in motivating people to meet the requirements of the future.

A sense of purpose inspires people to self-motivate.

When inspiring others, you are not just creating change; you're also illuminating it. And the more you can foster an intrinsic pressure to keep moving toward a new possibility, the easier the change will happen.

If you want to be a purpose-driven leader to inspire others, you have to define and communicate the reason that the company/project/program exists. Like everything else we've discussed, focus is key. We have daily opportunities in our work to keep ourselves, and everyone else, focused on a higher calling. Pink offered this point to me in an interview: "We've neglected the importance of purpose in our organizations. In the typical staff meeting you spend 45 minutes talking about how people do things or what they're supposed to do. Instead, spend four minutes talking about the why. What's the purpose of this enterprise? Why do we get up every day and work hard? Try spending even four minutes on purpose—on the why—and 41 minutes on the how and the what."[6]

Drawing attention to the why, and linking it to each individual's role, has a real impact on behavior and outcomes. Plus, it makes work a lot more interesting. Of course there's a neuroscience aspect too, as you've no doubt deduced. We are helping others to create new mental maps by focusing on solutions and creating attention density around positive insights. We are also enhancing rewards for status (being part of something important), certainty (identifying where we are headed), and relatedness (belonging to a team).

It's also why vision is critical for leaders, as we'll discuss in the next chapter.

This Is Heady Stuff, but Not Hard to See

When I first began learning about neuroleadership it seemed like a lot to digest. Frankly, it is. The good news is that even knowing the highlights is beneficial—and intriguing! The research findings make intuitive sense and validate human behavior that we observe in ourselves and in others throughout the workplace.[7]

Understanding how your brain operates gives you a broader and deeper perspective. Neuroscience explains why you might get a sense of overload as you read through a book, or why you might categorize an idea as "too hard" and mentally shut it out. It also explains why corporate reorganizations usually go so badly. Neuroscience takes common behaviors out of the personal and puts them into the biological, creating a different problem to solve with an opportunity for fresh solutions. It's acceptable and natural to feel the way we do; we are neither purposefully intractable nor personally inadequate. We're human. And given what we now know, we can approach change in an enlightened way.

Ultimately, what excites me the most is that neuroscience uncovers the potential that we can easily overlook in ourselves. It can help all of us become true inspirational forces for positive change and to understand the possibilities in ourselves and in our relationship to others.

Key Takeaways from Chapter 9

1. Neuroscience findings are revealing intriguing aspects of how the human brain processes information, makes decisions, and manages change. We know that the brain creates neural circuits—mental maps—that form the basis for our thoughts and perceptions. Each person's mental maps are unique.
2. Our prefrontal cortex, or the executive portion of our brain, is where our short-term thoughts and complex decision making occur. This is where the brain does its heavy lifting. Long-term memory (i.e., ingrained thoughts) requires less energy to store.
3. The brain is built for efficiency and energy conservation. When we confirm what we already know, energy is saved. When we confront ideas that conflict with current perceptions, we expend energy.

4. It's easier for us to form new connections in the brain than to change existing ones. When we create new mental maps that result in insights, we have a surge of adrenaline and often feel excited to take action. However, this feeling quickly wears off if we don't jump on it.

5. We sustain change by keeping our focus on the new insight. When we apply attention density—frequency, intensity, and deliberation—we are most likely to hardwire the new perspective into the brain, where it's stored as long-term memory.

6. To influence others, we must be mindful of the human brain's organizing principle of threat versus reward around status, certainty, autonomy, relatedness, and fairness. By staying on the reward side of these factors, we allow our communications to be heard with greater clarity and less reactivity.

Ideas I Want to Try from Chapter 9:

_____

_____

_____

_____

_____

CHAPTER 10

From Vision to Visionary

One afternoon on a winter day in 2009 I sat down to begin coaching Dave, the functional head of corporate marketing in a global health-care company that had just undergone a reorganization. The good news from all this change was that Dave's division had inherited a larger team of product marketers. The bad news was that both his existing team and his new team were on edge from the recent changes. They were worried about job security, career opportunities with an expanded team, and how Dave would manage through this transition so that the division would emerge stronger. Everyone liked Dave personally, but he was known for being in the weeds and not necessarily a proactive communicator. If you wanted to know what was going on, you had to hunt him down and ask directly. Otherwise, you might not hear from him for weeks.

When Dave and I began our work together, I asked him to tell me his vision for his new, combined team. He answered by parroting the company goal statement, which had been rolled out with much fanfare. He seemed pleased that he had remembered it. So I pushed back and asked again, "What is *your* vision? What is going to make your newly formed team energized to come to work every day? What is this team's role specifically in supporting the company goals?"

Dave stopped for a minute and admitted he hadn't thought of it. As a functional head, he didn't think it was his job to set a vision. It was then that I knew exactly where to begin our coaching.

Vision: It's for Every Leader

Dave's take on vision didn't make him an outlier; he was in the norm. In the day-to-day of work life, vision falls to the bottom of the list. It's considered a nice-to-have. Many leaders assume that vision is the purview of the very top. Senior executives expect to be involved in the company's vision, but not to lead it. Only CEOs know that vision is their job.

Vision, as it turns out, is much more egalitarian than totalitarian. All leaders can benefit from having a compelling vision (and it benefits aspiring leaders as well).

Vision is one of those barely tangible characteristics of executive presence that has great resonance. While we spot it immediately when it's there—often by calling someone strategic or forward-looking—we are not sure what's missing when it's absent. A client of mine once lamented that his executive team couldn't "hold their own" with the board. As we analyzed what that comment actually meant, it came down to their inability to articulate vision.

Visionaries run the teams everyone wants to work on.

As an employee, you know which leaders have vision. They run the teams everyone wants to work on. They are the CEOs people drop everything to follow. They create a reality that we clamor to be a part of. They personalize our work effort. I've been on teams with visionary leaders and felt I was changing the world, even if the rest of the company was falling apart around me. Sometimes it's the CEO who sets that vision. Other times it's a team leader. In great companies, visions start at the top and cascade down, to distinct teams that translate the vision from their unique perspective. Everyone has a part.

Alternatively, visionless leaders are in danger of cultivating teams with a sense of *anomie,* a concept proposed by French sociologist Emile Durkheim in the late 1800s that is best described as a feeling of purposelessness, of being disconnected from the whole.

Typically, people on such teams are biding time until something better comes along.

We covered the importance of purpose, certainty, and status in Chapter 9. It's not a big leap to see why vision enables all of these rewarding things, and more. I would argue that vision is necessary in a post–Knowledge Age era where information is readily available, cheap, unreliable, and frustratingly agnostic. We're drowning in data. When I started in PR, we talked about controlling the message. Today, that's a joke. At best, you can influence the message.

With so much information to process, we are not getting better at making decisions; we're getting worse. In *How We Decide,* Jonah Lehrer uses the case of back surgery to demonstrate this point.[1] For years, doctors approached back pain (which occurs in a notoriously complex area of the body and is difficult to diagnose) by surveying symptoms and generally prescribing rest as a wait-and-see approach. Most cases of back pain go away on their own when patients allow their body to heal. Today, doctors have the ability to use cutting-edge imaging technology to see into the patient's lower back and discover various areas of the region that may be causing pain. Often, surgery is prescribed. However, doctors are getting worse at treating back pain, not better. The new interventions don't appear to be alleviating the symptoms overall. The technology gives doctors a wealth of information about possible causes of back pain, but in general, back pain is as common, as severe, and as long-lasting today as it was 50 years ago. Back surgeons, just like the rest of us, can be overloaded with information and fail to find vital context and direction from it.

In the workplace, a vision helps the leader, and everyone else, figure out what's important. A vision provides context amidst chaos. We need data plus context to make decisions that are useful, relevant, and aligned with the organization's overall goals. As Lehrer notes, the human brain can only manage at most seven variables at a time, and when we get overloaded, we latch on to one or two items that may or may not be the most relevant.

Vision setting as a methodology and a process is important, but it's not what this book is about. Instead, I'm going to cover your role as the carrier of the vision—the *visionary*. Every leader can and should be a visionary. (After all, what's the alternative?)

Visionaries: No Magical Powers, but a Certain Something . . .

The word *visionary* sounds big. It conjures images of geniuses, seers, and iconoclasts, but not so much Bob in the accounting office. Ask managers if they consider themselves visionaries. Most will say "no." Now ask them if they'd like to be. Most will say, "Who wouldn't?" or "Why not?"

Every single person reading this book has the potential to be visionary. There's no magic behind it. It just requires time and attention—and an acknowledgment that if you want a strong presence, vision is worth the effort to develop and communicate. As shown in Figure 10-1, there are four aspects to becoming visionary in your daily work life, whether as the CEO of a multibillion-dollar conglomerate or as Bob toiling away on the annual audit. What makes visionaries visionary is their ability to be aspirational and personal, while also articulating a vision that is shared and active. Consider how you can incorporate each of these qualities into the normal gyrations of your day. I've yet to meet a leader who lacks the ability to be visionary. You just have to make it a priority.

Visionaries are aspirational and personal, while creating a vision that is shared and active.

A Visionary Is Aspirational

The first part of being a visionary is keeping your head up. Visionaries are positive, which makes everyone else feel positive. They encourage

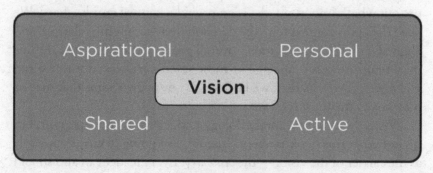

Figure 10-1. Elements of a visionary.

potential. They see the same problems that everyone sees, but they also see solutions. When times are bad, their vision acts as a compass to help a team stick together and find a way to the other side.

In *Good to Great,* Jim Collins discusses how high-performing companies have a core ideology that is enduring and value-driven and has intrinsic importance to employees.[2] This ideology—not financial performance or competitive position— is a company's reason for being. It's a higher calling, a purpose that people can buy into.

> *A company's reason for being shouldn't be about financial performance or trumping competitors. A vision is a higher calling.*

As you consider how to shape your vision into something that can be communicated, keep in mind that there's a difference between vision and goals. Consider the following statements:

— Increase our performance by 25 percent.
— Crush the giant in our industry.
— Create a product that will become the No. 1 choice in the market.
— Become the fastest-growing company in our sector.

These may be acceptable strategic goals, but are they truly visionary?

On the other hand, your vision can rise above the market fray when you describe it like this:

— Set a standard for innovation and risk taking.
— Exemplify how to balance profitability with social responsibility.
— Be a destination workplace known for leadership development.
— Bring happiness to our customers.
— Save lives.

As the visionary, your role is to tailor the vision so that it is meaningful to your team—whether it's the whole company or just two people. (Or it could be an outward vision to an industry or marketplace if that's your domain.) Strategic goals are critical for moving behavior in a common direction, but they don't inspire the same deep commitment as a vision. Great visions are engaging and inclusive. They support the concept of "flow"; that is, when people are exposed to a great vision, they want to invest themselves psychically in it. Rather than create a sense of us versus them, great visions create assurance that everyone is contributing to the whole. Think back on David Rock's SCARF model (discussed in Chapter 9). Great visions reduce threats to status, certainty, autonomy, relatedness, and fairness. Even if we disagree with the vision, we never feel excluded by it.

One last note: A great vision benefits everyone equitably. I hear a lot of vision statements from entrepreneurs, for example, about growing a market-leading business. Often this means that there are a few people at the top who stand to gain a lot, but then there's a steep drop-off in monetary reward for the rest of the folks toiling away at work. Be cautious that your vision doesn't disproportionately benefit a few.

Let's go back to the story that began this chapter. Dave, the corporate marketing head, decided to formulate a vision where both his former and newly acquired teams felt included. Because the pharmaceutical company where he worked was going through considerable change, with more to come, he also wanted to create an umbrella shelter where his group could have a core purpose, even when the rest of the company capitulated. The company was about improving the lives of others, and his marketing group had a unique role in developing and distributing messages to patients in need of their products. Dave's vision was to use the most creative marketing in the industry to bring awareness to people whose lives could be improved through his company's pharmaceutical products. He described his goal in terms of a team member looking back 10 years from now and saying, "That was the most innovative and successful work I ever produced. And I did it for the best possible reasons—saving lives!"

A Visionary Makes It Personal

Visionaries take their visions personally. It almost always starts with leaders looking inward to their deepest thoughts about what's important. It's a contemplative exercise of balancing what's right for the larger group, the community in which the company exists, and the leader's personal values and ambitions. Certainly for entrepreneurs and CEOs of closely held companies, what the leader can get behind has to be a key factor. If a CEO doesn't want fast growth, he will never be a credible advocate for a vision that includes a meteoric rise. People will see right through it.

Visionary leaders embody their vision through their presence. Their intentions support it and their actions prove it. A corporate vision can, though rarely, bubble up from the bottom or evolve organically from a big event. But it will go nowhere if the leader doesn't feel it in her bones. Leaders provide the pas-

> *A vision will go nowhere unless the leader feels it in her bones.*

sion, energy, and consistency to make a vision real for others. Visions can easily get lost in busy schedules or unexpected market detours; it's up to the leader to remind people what the group, team, or company is all about.

Tony Hsieh, the CEO of Zappos, certainly knows the importance of embodying a vision.[3] Zappos.com is one of the top online retailers in the country. In 2009, Amazon bought the company for more than $1.2 billion. But for 10 years before that, Hsieh saw Zappos through some of the most difficult market conditions possible for an online company. Nearly running out of cash on multiple occasions, the company was kept alive only by Hsieh's own funds. (At one point Hsieh had to sell his apartment in a desperate fire sale to keep the lights on.) His secret for greatness? An unwavering commitment to providing the ultimate customer experience. For Hsieh, that vision is intensely, deeply personal. At times, the decisions he made to maintain the vision seemed risky, if not downright financially crazy, such as the decision to warehouse inventory to improve customer satisfaction when the company was flat broke. But it worked. Zappos is not only preternaturally booming, it's so well known for its unique culture and strong corporate vision that when you Google the term "core values," the top links returned always include Zappos. (For a list of the Zappos core values, see the sidebar.)

‖‖

Zappos Core Values

1. Deliver WOW Through Service
2. Embrace and Drive Change
3. Create Fun and a Little Weirdness
4. Be Adventurous, Creative, and Open-Minded
5. Pursue Growth and Learning
6. Build Open and Honest Relationships with Communication
7. Build a Positive Team and Family Spirit
8. Do More with Less
9. Be Passionate and Determined
10. Be Humble

‖‖

Among leaders I work with, the biggest excuse for not being more visionary is that it takes time. And it does take time—not in quantity, but in quality. Determining what you truly want your team, or yourself, to represent takes introspection. It requires you to turn off the busyness in your life and to simply think. You have to quiet your mind to let your brain use its full capacity and allow the *Aha!* moment to occur. You may not need even a full day to formulate your vision, but it's a different kind of time spent. However, the payoff is immense.

One of my favorite examples of visioning comes from Bill Gates and his famous "think week." Each year when he was running Microsoft, he would go away for one full week alone just to remove interruptions and to think. He would read dozens of papers from Microsoft employees about trends and product ideas, as well as digest scores of outside research. Rather than keep his process behind the scenes, he talked openly about "think week," with both internal and external audiences. He wanted everyone to see how seriously he took this strategic time to craft his vision for Microsoft.

Anyone can replicate this idea. Can't do a full week? Do a "think day." Take Bill Gates's lead and be transparent about it. If you communicate how important having time to think is to you, it shows others how seriously you believe in your vision. This vision is not just a few words on a plaque somewhere, but a living, breathing purpose that guides your decisions.

People will follow your lead. If you want to be a visionary, you have to believe in the path with every ounce of who you are. It *is* personal.

A Visionary Creates Shared Understanding

For vision to inspire and mobilize, it must be shared among the group. Otherwise, it is more of a private goal than a group vision. And while the leader must personally buy in and believe, others must personally invest as well. Sharing a vision is never as easy as it seems. Here's what usually happens:

Step 1. A person or elite group of people develops a vision.
Step 2. The vision is announced to a larger group.
Step 3. Everyone is expected to embrace the vision for its
       magnificence.
Step 4. The vision fades to the background.

Truly visionary leaders use their presence to encourage others to be part of the vision. It's like developing trust: People have to elect to come toward a vision—it can't be pushed on them. If you push too hard, it begins to feel like coercion, and people will shut out your vision entirely.

> People come toward a vision. Similar to trust, it can't be forced.

As a leader trying to get people to embrace a vision, one of the best approaches is to open up your thinking and invite others to help define the vision—*before* your mind is made up. It can't be a symbolic, after-the-fact gesture. The great management guru Peter Senge talks of "learning organizations" combining advocacy with inquiry.[4] In this approach, leaders advocate for their position and then inquire how others feel about it. Instead of defending their ideas as objections emerge, leaders continually sharpen them while soliciting other ideas until everyone in the room has offered input.

I've taken this process a step further as it relates to inspiring a group to set a vision. (It also works beautifully for any situation that

Figure 10-2.   "DIAL in" model for buy-in.

requires that all-important buy-in.) I call it the "DIAL in" process. The basic steps are *describe, invite, acknowledge,* and *leverage* (see Figure 10-2).

To see how DIAL in works around vision, let's return to Dave's story. His team vision is to bring awareness to people whose lives could be improved through the most creative marketing in the pharmaceutical industry. Before he rolled out his vision with much hoopla and a red bow, he first took the idea to his group and followed the DIAL in steps.

Step 1: Describe
Dave shared his thinking with his team members, taking care to fully divulge his thought process. He let them know how important a solid team vision was and how he had arrived at a potential vision for the group. He made sure to let them know that he wanted it to be a vision that supported the corporate mission and, at the same time, held special meaning for team members themselves, no matter what happened around them.

Step 2: Invite
Dave then asked the group, "What am I missing?" and "How can we make this idea better?" As people began to present thoughts,

Dave was careful not to defend his own original vision. He didn't talk much at all during this process, except to probe further and to help others clarify their thoughts. At all times, Dave made sure to tease out the thinking behind people's statements.

Step 3: Acknowledge

Acknowledgment was a concept first introduced in Chapter 7, in the discussion of empathy, which is another key emotion related to gaining buy-in. Whenever possible, Dave made sure to acknowledge other people's points—whether or not he agreed with them. Simply hearing Dave say, "I can see why you would say that" or "You've put a lot of thought into this topic" helped team members to understand that Dave was taking the time to put himself in their shoes.

Step 4: Leverage

As new ideas flowed in the room, they began to build off one another. Dave facilitated by putting disparate ideas together to leverage the thoughts into a more and more relevant, inspiring vision for the whole group. He had to pay sharp attention to avoid getting overly invested in any one idea. Rather, he functioned as the architect of the group's combined wisdom. As he formed these ideas into a coherent picture, he went back to the beginning and described what he was seeing and hearing—starting the cycle again.

* * *

Finally, Dave wrapped up by thanking his team members for their thoughts and time. He made sure everyone felt heard and had provided input, and he promised a quick follow-up. By the end, he had agreement and some enthusiastic supporters for his vision.

I encourage you to try this process to create a shared vision, or as a buy-in exercise anytime you have a new idea you want to introduce. It sounds simple enough, but here's a warning: Be prepared to fight against the impulse to defend your ideas as people raise questions. You've already invested in your own vision by virtue of the time and energy you've expended to get there. Your neural circuits are firing and you'll likely resist anything that counters your position. However, if you begin to defend your position (often with a lot of "*but* sandwiches," such as "That's a good idea, but . . . I see why you'd say that, but . . .), you'll wind up with a room full of people passively nodding their heads. No one is going to stand up to the boss when his mind is already made up. There's nothing to gain and lots to lose.

I've used this exercise frequently in workshops with seasoned CEOs. One leader will present an idea about which she feels strongly. A few others will act as the audience, providing alternate takes on it. Keep in mind, these are people who are accustomed to having the last (and loudest) word on the ideas they generate. Invariably, the person acting as the leader will admit that it was killing her to hold back her vociferous defense of her ideas. It's good to learn how easy (or difficult) it is to hear opposing positions, and how to have the self-control to inquire about the other person's thought processes rather than relentlessly promote your own.

A visionary leader wants to hear how others think and feel. She knows that the power in a vision is that it is shared—and that the sum is always greater than the individual parts.

A Visionary Keeps It Active

The first three attributes of a visionary are the most commonly considered. Most leaders know they must be able to believe and share an inspiring vision. We can almost always muster the energy for that. It's creative and positive and neatly ephemeral. The vision is completed. Box checked.

Visionary leaders, however, know that for a vision to mean anything, it must be active. It must be woven into the nuances of everyday life. Sometimes you must explain it until you're blue in the face! It requires commitment to a process. No surprise, this is the part of visioning that begins to feel less like fun and more like hard work.

Visionary leaders know that vision is meaningless unless it's active and alive.

Often, I see this element of a visionary underdeveloped or omitted entirely. When I'm coaching leaders on this point, I can watch them zone out. Or I'll get a quick dismissal. *Yes, yes, we're doing that.* We all want to believe that if we know our own vision and mention it occasionally, everyone will remember it. Frustratingly repetitive as it may seem, vision must be reinforced constantly—not just through words but *actions,* which are far more revealing. For a quick check on how clearly the group sees your vision, ask your people to write down what they believe the vision is, then compare everyone's answers. You'll likely be surprised by what you find.

If you want to be visionary, make a plan to keep the vision alive. Have it become a personal tagline of sorts and weave it into conversations and presentations at every opportunity. Every company meeting—even weekly—should reinforce your vision and show how you are *living* it. Give examples of a company milestone, or point out a particular team member's efforts that align with the vision and the strategy. In fact, put that on the agenda! All of your team members should know how their efforts contribute to the vision. Every conversation with an employee should be viewed as an opportunity to reinforce the vision. Post the company's vision throughout the office and on your website so that customers and partners know it as well. Zappos posts its vision on its website, along with videos of staff members talking about what it means to them, and the concepts are woven into recruiting, hiring, and management practices at the company. All new hires have the company's core values ingrained in them during training. (To weed out the nonbelievers, Zappos even offers a $2,000 payout at the end of training for anyone who doesn't fully buy in and wants to *leave.*) Company celebrations and employee awards are built around the core values. Tony Hsieh even wrote a book about them. At Zappos, the core values are very much a living, breathing part of the culture.

For Dave, our case-study leader who, as you recall, wasn't an effusive communicator, keeping his vision active meant making a personal plan and strategizing around the ways he could incorporate vision into his normal workday. There were more opportunities than he realized when he considered that being a visionary wasn't an addition to his job but was a big part of it.

The Presence to Keep Your Head Up

In the day-to-day world of heads-down work, visionaries are the ones who keep their heads up, and along with them, everyone else's. Visionaries are disciplined to keep looking forward, to tomorrow and the next day and the next. They gain perspective by rising above the chaos to discern patterns from disparate parts. They bring the complex to a simple level and communicate it in a way that makes others want to hear and remember. Their executive presence connotes forward motion and optimism.

A vision doesn't have to be grand or innovative. It just has to be relevant and meaningful—and always a priority.

Case Study in Visionary Leadership: Niki Leondakis

For me, one memorable example of visionary leadership is Niki Leondakis, former COO of San Francisco–based Kimpton Hotels & Restaurants, which operates luxury boutique hotels throughout the United States and Canada, including Hotel Monaco properties. The company was honored by *Fortune* magazine in 2009 as a best place to work and has earned accolades for its commitment to employee development and social responsibility. If you have ever been to one of Kimpton's properties, you know their reputation for being uniquely über stylish and slightly playful, with a high level of customer care. You feel hip and pampered just sitting in the lobby.

I interviewed Niki for my *Entrepreneur.com* column in February 2009 as part of a series on how leaders inspire in an economic downturn.[5] The hospitality industry rides the market ebbs and flows like a small dinghy at sea, and I thought a luxury hotel that continues to thrive in a tough market would have some answers. I asked Niki how she kept her team of 6,500 employees at 41 properties focused and positive during times of uncertainty. What I found was that Niki had a keen understanding of her vision and her role as a visionary.

"I consider myself a hope giver," Niki explained. "My style is based on honesty and compassion. People need to know what to expect from a leader and trust in you to tell them what's going on."

Niki described her process for keeping the vision alive. It's a firm commitment she makes with herself that demonstrates the vision's importance to her leadership. Each year she travels the country to visit every hotel and restaurant to talk with employees. As she described it, the method is "like painting the Golden Gate Bridge." As soon as the job is complete, it starts again. She uses this time to reinforce the corporate culture and core values, and to hear straight from employees their perspectives about Kimpton.

During the recession that followed the 2007 financial crisis, many leaders had a tendency to hunker down, adopting a perpetual wait-and-see policy. Niki took a different approach: "I scheduled an all-managers conference call and addressed the issue head-on. I tried to model the behavior I wanted our VPs to emulate and repeat throughout the company.

"We made a commitment to continue key meetings where we speak to, motivate, and inspire employees. We reduced the bells and whistles [at these meetings], but we didn't cancel them," she explained. "I spoke to the general managers about what's going on and how to rise above what they don't have control over. I challenged them to use this opportunity to create their defining moments as leaders."

One hesitation I frequently hear about visioning is that the leader doesn't know what's around the bend. He's afraid to put a stake in the ground. This fear is compounded during reorganizations and times of change. Niki had this take: "I tell the truth. There is always certainty in something. I acknowledge the unknown, but can say with absolute certainty no matter what happens, we will not lose our integrity or compromise our culture or change who we are."

For Niki, it was important to provide context to employees—to share her own perspective from the patterns she could see from her position. She showed in specific terms how Kimpton's situation compared to others in the hospitality industry. And she used stories to share Kimpton's own history of the company's toughest year—not 2009, but 2001, when it faced both a paralyzing recession and the death of its founder. Niki reminded people: "We've survived and thrived in tougher times than this, and we can do it again."

Part of demonstrating vision is through priorities—what goes and what stays. Niki made sure to back up her vision with actions that demonstrated her commitment. When the company needed to reduce costs, every employee down to the front line was asked to brainstorm ways to help. With broader buy-in, the changes were easier to accept. She launched a contest to emphasize the company's value of customer care by awarding employees for creating the best Kimpton moment, as judged by guests. She spoke repeatedly about the need for putting "you first, family second, work third," so that employees didn't become overwhelmed by stress—even to the point of offering a self-care workshop during the brunt of the recession.

And to support Kimpton's policy of social responsibility, including environmental stewardship, the company maintained its charitable commitment levels while other businesses cut back.

Niki offered this advice for leaders: "No matter how stressed you are, deal with it privately. Maintain a positive attitude and it will come through in your communications and body language. If you allow yourself to focus on the negative and spiral into fear, do whatever you have to do to get your frame of mind positive and focused on what you can control."

Every step of the way, Niki outwardly communicated her thinking and linked the company's actions to its values. She talked about her need to communicate tenaciously and to never, ever assume that people understand the situation just because the leaders do. She was tireless and committed, but also joyful and authentic. With leaders like Niki, it's not a surprise that Kimpton has enjoyed the success it has. In 2010, it opened its 50th hotel and was named No. 1 in customer satisfaction by Market Metrix.

Try for Less Futurist and More Focus

I began this chapter by discussing how important vision is in companies, and how it is within reach of every leader. Niki Leondakis's example illustrates that vision isn't about grand clairvoyance but a commitment, followed by repeatable practices: all at once aspirational, personal, shared, and active. There are a few ideas here that you can put into practice. As it turns out, being visionary isn't all that sexy. Bob in accounting has everything he needs. As does Dave in marketing. And you, too.

Key Takeaways from Chapter 10

1. Being a visionary isn't just for CEOs, futurists, or industry gurus. All leaders can and should view their role as a visionary for their domain.

2. Visionaries communicate visions that are aspirational. Great visions bring groups together around a common and enduring higher purpose, not short-lived strategic or financial goals.
3. Visionaries take their visions personally. They have to invest with their hearts and souls, or no one else will feel a deep commitment.
4. Visionaries create a shared vision. They create buy-in by allowing others to co-create the vision through a DIAL in process, where there's a cycle to *describe, invite, acknowledge,* and *leverage* ideas.
5. Visionaries keep the vision active. Visions should be woven into the fabric of daily office interactions or they are quickly forgotten. This is usually the part leaders would rather skip, as it can feel repetitive and mundane—but it's key.

Ideas I Want to Try from Chapter 10:

_____

_____

_____

_____

_____

CHAPTER 11

Declarations Create Possibilities

"We're going to make history together today."

That's what Steve Jobs said when he first took the stage at the Macworld 2007 event I described in Chapter 1. That one simple statement changed the energy in the room. He piqued excitement. Imagine if he'd begun as many speeches do: "I'd like to share some exciting updates with you about the company." Not quite the same effect, is it?

Language holds power. When it's filled with confidence and passion, and backed by our authentic presence, it can transform us. Remember in Chapter 2 when you practiced slumping in your chair, a negative posture, while speaking words that were genuinely positive? You felt the impact in your body and in your mood.

In this final part of I-Presence, we are covering how to inspire with your presence, whether through a vision, a process of change, or your daily communications. Your presence is conveyed by the way you communicate in total. Part of that is through the words you choose. This chapter delves into the realm of language. In essence, inspiring through language is about painting a picture of

Declarations are powerful. It's tough to inspire by playing small.

what the future could be. It includes the use of declarations, exactly as Steve Jobs demonstrated with his "We're going to make history" statement. Inspirational language steps us into a bigger game. After all, it's tough to inspire by playing small.

For some of you reading this chapter, this type of bold communication won't feel like your style at all. And yes, authenticity is still the goal of this book. I suggest that you suspend any initial reactions and let the ideas marinate. Being declarative involves both style and mind-set. Declarations can force us out of our comfort zone. As we learned in Chapter 9, our brain chemistry automatically resists uncertainty, even when the end result can be exceedingly positive.

In this chapter and the next, I'll highlight the best communications practices of leaders that anyone can emulate, regardless of industry or position. Declarations are our starting point. These ideas aren't difficult to grasp and buy into. Finding what methods work for you and putting them into practice is usually the harder part. As you've done throughout the book, take what works for you and try it out. You don't need to do everything, or to do it all one way. As you read on, you'll discover that there are many ways to inspire.

Declarations Broken Down

What makes a declaration so powerful? In a way, it's a public frame for our intentions. Declarations create and clarify vision for others and ourselves. They help to define that all-important sense of purpose around our work.

A declaration is a promise of something more, of greatness. Declarations are made individually and shared. Declarations inspire followership.

Simply put, a declaration is stating, "I (or we) will do _____." The blank is all yours, and only yours, to fill in.

Declarations are compelling, ambitious, strong, direct, and enticingly risky. They show confidence in oneself and in the power of the collective. They force us to push ourselves and play on a bigger stage. They provide a rallying point that brings a group together.

Declarations are all around us. You can find them in social

movements and political campaigns. The civil rights movement declared "We shall overcome." Think of the 2008 Obama campaign's "Yes, we can," or the implicit declaration in Reagan's 1984 slogan "It's morning again in America." Declarations open up possibilities. They change our viewpoint. John F. Kennedy proclaimed in 1962 in his speech at Rice University that the United States would put a man on the moon before the end of the decade. Kennedy's bold claim precipitated a cascade of new thoughts and actions. Ultimately, the goal was realized.

We have many examples of compelling declarations from American leaders or billionaire entrepreneurs. We expect them and gladly accept them from larger-than-life personalities. But similar to vision, declarations aren't the strict purview of futurists or iconoclasts. We all can incorporate declarative statements in our communications when we want to put a stake in the ground, create change, or get noticed. Declarations can be grand and idealistic, such as "We'll make history." They can be specific and measurable, such as "We will surpass our fourth quarter goal by 10 percent." Declarations can be personal ("I will write a book this year") or group-oriented ("We will out-market our competitor").

Declarations are compelling, ambitious, strong, direct, and enticingly risky.

The content is secondary. The belief and commitment are primary.

Declarations are a personal communications tool that everyone reading this book can use today. It doesn't matter where you are on the path of leadership. In fact, you could argue, declarations make leaders. People who boldly put themselves out there are more interesting, memorable, and charismatic. They exude presence. We admire their pluck and daring. We orient ourselves differently around them.

I believe that declarations are the most effective and underused communications tool in companies today. Many studies have shown that worker satisfaction is tied to the feeling of being part of something larger than oneself. It is that sense of purpose that creates drive, as outlined by author Daniel Pink. Spend even a small amount of time in corporations and you can see that we are in dire need of leaders to chart the way.

"I Don't Do Risky," and Other Excuses

Inevitably, when I bring up declarations in a workshop, people are squirming in their seats, bursting to tell me why this is a crazy idea. They are uncomfortable making bold proclamations—out loud—that they might not be able to live up to. They worry about losing credibility. They live their life by the motto that it's better to under-promise and overdeliver. They play it safe.

I am not advocating making fanciful declarations that you can't possibly meet. I'm suggesting that declarations have a pivotal role in pushing others and ourselves toward larger objectives that are just within our grasp if we strive. Declarations are about inspiring others, using our personal influence, and showing confidence in our own abilities.

We live in a world where the de facto standard is a workplace of masterful hedgers. (The cultural expression "CYA" emerged for a reason.) We walk around hedging our bets and making watered-down declarations all the time. It's neither interesting nor inspiring. And it's a missed opportunity to be more.

> *We walk around hedging our bets and making watered-down declarations all the time.*

Consider these common workplace statements. What are your reactions to them?

Hedge	Declaration
If everything breaks our way, we can hit our quarterly number.	We will hit our number this quarter.
I think I might be able to streamline our financial processes.	I commit to streamlining our financial processes by year's end.
This new product just might change the nature of our industry.	We are going to change the face of our industry with this new product.
I'm going to try my best to exceed my development goals this year.	I will exceed my development goals this year.

When you see the statements side by side, the difference is abundantly clear. You can't get very excited about a statement filled with caveats. On the other hand, the declarations help you envision the goal.

When I videotape leaders in my coaching sessions, the power of language and how it is used hits home. When they see themselves littering key statements with "I think" or "I might," they realize how much of their own influence they are leaving on the table. Just making the tweak to "I will" or even "I plan to" completely changes the tone of their discourse. Suddenly, they're not just informing but inspiring.

It's Okay to Fail, but Not to Hide

In Chapter 6, I talked about how failure can deepen trust if it is confronted and used to improve. I want to expand upon that thought.

You don't lose your credibility from failure but from how you handle it.

Declarations do involve risk. It's a fact that if you make a commitment you might not meet it. You have a zero percent chance at failing at something you don't try. Yes, you might fail. People do it all the time. You don't lose your credibility from failure itself but from how you handle the failure. You can fail; you just can't hide.

Consider this common workplace scenario: Your company rolls out a new initiative with a daring claim. Perhaps the CEO herself states that the company will achieve said goal. Months go by with no further word on the initiative. Eventually, the rank and file begins to wonder what happened. Easy answer: The goal wasn't met, the company got distracted, and leadership hoped the issue would blow over. The CEO is embarrassed to discuss the failed initiative. But by now she's on to other things—and she hopes everyone else is, too.

In fact, of course everyone remembers! And credibility is damaged. More important, an opportunity to inspire achievement has been wasted.

Humans understand failure. We give permission to our leaders to fail. As we discussed in Chapter 6, hearing how other people struggle actually helps us connect with them. We simply expect accountability. Imagine the difference if instead of hiding, the CEO had stood up to say, "We didn't meet our goal. Here's what I could have done better. Here's what the company could have done better.

Here's how we are adjusting the goal with this new information to ensure success next time."

This narrative plays out repeatedly in politics, too. Candidates make big campaign promises that are watered down in the legislative process. "No new taxes" is a common one. Then inevitably, Congress passes some form of a tax, even if it's not an income tax increase. At that point, the politician has an opportunity to increase or erode his trust level with constituents. If he backpedals on his campaign promise—"Well, I never said no taxes. What I meant was no new *income* tax"—then his followers lose faith in him. However, if he stands up and says, "I did make that promise, and it was a personal mission of mine. When I saw the latest deficit numbers I had to make a tough decision that involved a form of a tax. Here's why I believe it was the right thing to do for our district . . . ," voters may still be disappointed, but trust can be preserved and even built.

Here's another point to consider. When we put declarations out in the world, even if we don't meet them, we advance further than we would have otherwise. We learn more. And we put ourselves on a broader path.

Now, for those of you still squirming in your seats with discomfort, let's acknowledge that there are people who get a reputation for making audacious claims they can never achieve. Our *Declarations are authentic when you believe in them and when you have the ability to make them happen.*

radar goes up around these people. We may get sucked in one time because we so want to believe in them, but we learn quickly. This kind of bombastic style is not authentic presence. Your declarations are authentic when *you* truly believe they are possible. They are credible when you have the *capability* to achieve them.

||||||||||||||||||||||||||||||||||||||||||||||||||||||||||||||||||||||||||||||||||||||||||||||||||||||||

What's Your Declaration?

We can all use more declarations in our lives. Why not start now? Take this opportunity to make a personal declaration. For inspiration, consider these questions:

- What would you like to achieve this year?
- What to-do item have you been carrying in your head and waiting for the right time to act on?

- What's an audacious goal you can make for your life?
- What feels like a right next step for you?
- What could you commit to doing that would change everything?

When you've decided what your declaration will be, make it real by writing it down on paper.

I will commit to _____.

Now say it out loud. Take a moment to reflect on it. Does it seem risky? What's at stake? What would hitting the goal feel like? Can you feel the excitement?

|||||||||||||||||||||||||||||||||||||||||||||||||||||||||||||||||||||||||||||||||||||||||||||||||||||||||||||

Finally, once you've settled on a declaration, consider how the world around you would benefit (or help you achieve it) if you communicated it. Whom would you share it with first? Perhaps start with friends and family, and then move on to your workplace. Or tell your boss what you're doing. Leaders may want to make the declaration first to their immediate team and then to the overall company. Once you get going, you'll find that the declaration feels more and more right, and sharing comes naturally. Outwardly communicating your declaration can bring buy-in and support. And as an added bonus, what gets shared is far more likely to be achieved.

Here's a personal experience where I was reminded of the power of declarations. Let's go back to 2003, when I was in the thick of running my PR firm. The market was slowly stabilizing from the technology recession and we were beginning to see some light at the end of the tunnel. It was still tough going for those of us selling marketing services. That's not where companies invest first. Maintaining our staff and our competitive position while we waited for the market to come back took everything my partner and I had. We diversified our services and entered new markets while servicing clients and selling like crazy. And in the middle of all of that, I had my first child.

As every mother and father knows, the first year that you are a parent the universe does a seismic shift—which manifests itself acutely for working mothers. You feel like a different person walking through a world that hasn't changed. You're trying to balance this new, pressing, and daunting responsibility for another human life with external responsibilities such as work, paying bills, and—let's face it—taking a shower and eating dinner. It's amazing and wonderful. All the while, your internal dialogue is frequently about how on earth you're going to pull this whole thing off.

For me, coming back to work after maternity leave presented a few challenges. First, neither my business partner nor I ever had a child before; in fact, only one other person in a company filled with women had children. I knew I was setting a precedent for how to balance it all. Several young women in the firm looking to their own future as working mothers remarked that they were watching me to see how it's done. (No pressure or anything.) Second, my business partner and I had decided that when I returned from maternity leave, I would make business development my sole focus. No more client work for me; instead, just sales. So in sum, I was coming back to a brand-new job with hard-to-reach goals that justified my existence. And everyone was watching.

I was excited, but anxious. I didn't know how to reconcile it all and meet my own expectations. I worried about failure. Fortunately, I was able to talk things over with my leadership coach, Clyde Northrop, group chair at Vistage International. Clyde gave it to me straight. He said I needed to put myself out there and be bold. He encouraged me to stretch out of the comfortable and announce an audacious sales goal to the whole company in our all-staff meeting. We had always had sales targets, but they had no teeth. He helped me craft the most specific, measurable stretch goal the company had ever proposed.

When I returned to the office in January 2004, I stood up and announced my new role, declaring what I would achieve: "I will bring in four new clients this quarter and exceed our year-over-year sales by 20 percent." I willed myself to project it with confidence. And you can guess the rest of the story. I got rave reviews from our team about the session. We hit the goal, and that's how I managed sales from that point forward.

Seek Out Opportunities to Inspire

Every day in your job you have opportunities to inspire others and to push yourself. Start looking for chances to make declarations. Times when you need to inspire change, increase performance, or generate new ideas are obvious places to start (not to mention when you need to give yourself a solid kick in the pants).

Be bold. Fear of failure shouldn't deter you from making declarations to others or to yourself. As a friend once aptly put it: "Who wants to go sleepwalking through their life?"

If you've gotten this far in a book about presence, I'd say definitely not you.

Key Takeaways from Chapter 11

1. Language holds the power to transform others and ourselves. Declarations are bold statements of a promise of greatness. Declarations are both made individually and shared.
2. Anyone, at any level, can use more declarative language in communications. Leaders can use declarations to set a vision and inspire followership. Aspiring leaders can enhance their prospects for achieving success and getting noticed by using declarations.
3. Declarations can be idealistic, grand, individual, group-oriented, or measurable. The content is less important than the belief and commitment behind them.
4. One simple way to be more declarative in your daily work life is to stop hedging important statements with "I think" or "I might." Instead say, "I will."
5. Fear of failure shouldn't stop you from making declarations. We don't lose credibility from failure but from how we respond to failure. Furthermore, even if we don't hit our goal, we'll get a lot closer if we declare it.

Ideas I Want to Try from Chapter 11:

_____

_____

_____

_____

CHAPTER 12

Strategic Shock Value and Other Ways to Create Shining Moments

One of the harder aspects of leadership for many people is that being in the role means being in the spotlight. Constant pressure to be "on" at work can wear down even a natural extrovert. Sometimes it's tempting to run and hide. My own knee-jerk reaction when things get tough is to hunker down, eliminate distractions, and focus on carrying out solutions. I'll go there in a heartbeat because it's easy for me. While this is a perfect strategy for a solo contributor, for anyone leading a team, the difficult times are exactly when you need to stay out in front. I've learned the hard way (more than once) that if I hole myself up, I will have a much harder time getting everyone behind me when I return to the fray.

Avoiding the spotlight that's inherent to the leadership role benefits no one, least of all the leader. This chapter is about accepting the spotlight and learning to play on an ever-bigger stage.

> Avoiding the spotlight that's inherent in the leadership role benefits no one, least of all the leader.

Why is accepting the spotlight important for leaders? First of all, people expect it. We want our leaders to be a little stronger in their sense of purpose and more insightful and more visible than the average person.

After all, we look to our leaders for guidance and vision. Second, to communicate a message you first have to be heard. It's noisy out there, and given what we know about brain function, it's noisy *in* there, too. At times, being a few degrees from the mean and grabbing attention is the only way your point will rise above the din. Finally, it's human nature to look to our leaders for clues about our own fate. We analyze a leader's every gesture, searching for signs. (This is observed in humans and further down the primate chain. Baboons glance at their alpha male every 20 to 30 seconds to see what he's doing.[1]) It's that red blinking light effect of leadership again showing what's important. Followers create the stage—the leader simply takes it.

> *We pay more attention to what's happening up the hierarchical chain than down. Baboons glance at their alpha male every 20 to 30 seconds.*

The spotlight *is* on leaders, whether or not they expect or desire it. It's true whether you are the CEO, are in middle management, or have emerged as a team leader

So, if you have the spotlight, what are you doing with it? How can you use it to inspire other people? How can you reach a broader audience? What's the right amount of attention and what's too much?

In the previous chapter, I introduced declarations—inspirational tools that unlock positive potential. Using declarations sets you apart and draws attention to you, no doubt. In this chapter, I'm going a step further with ways to create shining moments throughout the ordinary workday, for those times when you can readily seize the opportunity to establish presence.

Think of yourself as a walking billboard that demonstrates the kind of leader that you are. That billboard may be placed in the right venues, but if it's not well designed and looks similar to adjacent signs, it won't get noticed. This chapter is about optimizing your existing placements.

No Matter Where You Enter the Stage, Be Interesting When You Get on It

As a leader, or even an aspiring one, you are regularly in settings where you can inspire others. We've talked a lot in this book about meetings, but there are also networking events, client presentations, strategy sessions, and speaking engagements, to name a few. Since you must motivate others through communications, it's actually hard to find a time when you should *not* be inspiring.

Here's some good news. Part of being inspiring is simply being interesting. Having an impassioned point of view or a bold take on a situation is far better than the alternative—being taciturn and forgettable. A leader who plays it safe and stays under the radar inspires no one. There are times when shock is an effective strategy.

Inspiring is being interesting, whether it's a bold view, impassioned rhetoric, or even being shocking.

I'll admit that I'm a bit of a zealot, having worked with countless leaders—and listened to them address reporters, analysts, and public audiences. There is a lot of boring conversation happening out there. I don't know if it's the conventional wisdom that the nail that sticks up gets hammered down, or general fear of the spotlight, but most leaders elect to hug the middle of the road. (It's not that I found that leaders lacked interesting things to say when the curtain came down. They just held back when it counted the most. My job was coaching them to show more personality.)

It's one of the dirty little secrets about PR, and an anecdote I mentioned early in the book. While PR professionals dedicate most of their time developing newsworthy story angles and reaching out to reporters and media outlets, the real golden ticket is an interesting and engaging spokesperson. You can have a mediocre company with a charismatic spokesperson and get great press. I saw it happen all the time. On the contrary, a company blowing the financial doors off their hinges, but with a reticent spokesperson—that requires heavy PR lifting. Why? Interesting is inspiring. Reporters are energized to write more and readers want to learn more. More press equals more visibility, which means a bigger stage for the leader.

Consider another typical professional situation: the panel discussion at a conference or event. Most panels can induce narcolepsy. The speakers not only express common thoughts, but in an effort to be courteous, they reinforce the comments of the other panelists to show agreement. It's a middle-of-the-road land grab, and most of what's said is forgotten soon after the audience leaves the room. When we do hear that rare panelist who dares to stand out, she captures attention and gets flooded with questions afterward. The interesting panelist gets remembered and invited to do more panels. Another bigger stage created.

There's Bad Interesting and Good Interesting

It's hard to define exactly what makes a person inspiring or interesting. To a certain degree, *good interesting* is in the eye of the beholder. There's no magic to it. It's about authentic presence: being intentional, presenting our real selves, sharing stories, exposing vulnerability, or showing empathy. An interesting speaker can also be using humor or saying what everyone's thinking but won't verbalize.

Being *good interesting* means staying in alignment with our executive presence intention and bringing our full selves to our communications. It's about accepting the spotlight and using it to a greater and positive advantage.

On the flip side, as hard as good interesting is to define, it's remarkably easy to identify *bad interesting*. In no way am I advocating being outrageous for attention, misrepresenting yourself, taking the credit from deserving peers, grandstanding for personal gain, or always having to have the last and loudest word. But there's a wide distance between these behaviors and stepping into the spotlight gracefully and confidently so others take notice.

> *Workplace sensitivity is at play in the leadership spotlight. What flies on Wall Street may crash in the Midwest.*

Finally, workplace cultural sensitivity is also at play. Positive attention-seeking behavior that flies on Wall Street might be off-putting if you worked for an engineering firm in the Midwest. You have to know what the good-bad interesting boundaries are where you work and find a fit between them. (Just be mindful to factor the boundaries around the larger culture, not your own personal comfort level.)

‖‖

What's Good Interesting vs. Bad Interesting in Your Workplace?

Think of two or three engaging peers with a track record of success in your organization. (If you're the CEO, consider other top leaders at similar-size companies in your market.)

Observe them in action as much as you can in the typical workplace scenarios that are described throughout this chapter. (If you can't see them in person, search for presentations online.) What do they do that garners attention? What do they talk about? What does their presence convey?

Now think of two or three peers who have a reputation for grandstanding or being out for themselves. What do they do that creates this impression? What can you learn about your cultural boundaries from observing them?

‖‖

Shining Moments in the Daily Grind

To bring the concept of the *good interesting* down to a practical level, the rest of this chapter outlines typical workplace scenarios that create a presence spotlight. Most of the time, these opportunities come and go with little thought. I merely suggest that you consider them to be a chance to shine.

For each situation, there are recommended ways to use the platform to stand out, get noticed, establish your personal presence brand, and be seen as memorable and interesting. These suggestions incorporate ideas from various parts of the book and add new thoughts as well. It would be difficult to embrace all of the ideas here all of the time. Consider what fits for you, and then stretch yourself a little. Reframe a daily grind occurrence as an opportunity, a shining moment, and see what changes about your perspective and your practices.

Networking Events

Daily Grind People often approach networking events as a necessary evil for business or career development. A typical approach is to get it over with by conversing with the most easily approachable people and keeping an eye on your watch. If you manage to say your elevator pitch a few times, collect several business cards, and arrive home unscathed from awkward exchanges, you call it a success.

Go into networking events to help others, not to ask for something from them.

Shining Moment Take a different tack. Turn your purpose around. Your role is not to ask anyone for anything, but to help those who may benefit from your advice or your experience. When you bring down your self-orientation (remember the trust equation from Chapter 6), you not only boost trust but you set yourself apart from the majority of the people. Go into any room and any networking event with that aim in mind; you'll find it's easier to meet more new people.

- Don't just regurgitate prepared business sound bites. Bring your real self into the conversation and talk about interesting tidbits from your life. (If you both have kids or share a hobby, getting a conversation going is a slam-dunk.)
- Relate your own stories to those of the people you meet, remembering to mix confidence with vulnerability. There's already a ton of bragging at networking events, so don't add to it.
- Establish what master networker and author Keith Ferrazzi calls "conversational currency" by keeping up with current events, global trends, and pop culture so that you have multiple topics to discuss.[2] In one recent networking event, I talked about the economy of Iceland, the TV show *Mad Men,* Speaker of the House John Boehner, and a celebrity marriage rumor. You have to be ready to talk about whatever is interesting to the other person.
- When all else fails, remember that people love to talk about themselves. Ask great questions and practice empathic listening.

Internal Meetings

Daily Grind Meetings are among the most reviled aspects of corporate life. People typically do the minimum to prepare before a meeting, and when they are in a meeting, they regularly drift off, attend to their own to-do lists, or fiddle with their smartphones. Some minor points are beaten to the ground, while important topics remain unaddressed. Afterward, follow-up is notoriously unreliable. The general consensus is that most meetings are a waste of time.

Meetings offer ample opportunities to create a standout experience.

Shining Moment As discussed in Chapter 1, when I introduced the Intentionality Frame, meetings are the most common place where people show up as leaders. Just about every meeting holds an opportunity to convey your presence because, by design, every participant gets a turn in the spotlight. Because meetings are, in general, poorly run, there's ample room to be different and interesting whether you are the leader or a participant.

- If you are running the meeting, preface it by showing how you'll respect people's time. Send out an agenda and promise to keep the meeting to a specified length of time.
- Go into the meeting with your situational intention. What do you want the post-meeting hallway chitchat to be about? What emotion do you need to embody?
- Structure the meeting to focus not just on what needs to happen, but why it needs to be done. Create purpose by taking time to explain the why behind the agenda topics.
- Open up the meeting with ground rules and gain agreement to them. Establish ground rules for not checking phones, not piling on, sticking to core issues, and committing to follow up at the end. Reconfirm your commitment to ending the meeting on time if the rules are honored.
- Have some fun if the purpose is creativity or staff fraternity. Play music when people enter the room or have a team ritual to create camaraderie. Greg Stock at Vovici, whose story I shared in Chapter 2, keeps a poster of the corporate mascot, a lion, in the conference room. It gets high-fived by the team on the way out after big meetings, locker-room style.
- Model effective listening skills. Don't cut people off, and make sure you understood their points by rephrasing them. Listen fully instead of trying to think of a pithy reply.

- If you don't have anything additive to say, ask insightful questions. Questions often move the dialogue further along, and they stimulate those all-important *Aha!* moments.
- Use declarations for your commitments. Don't be wishy-washy; be clear about what you'll do, then follow through.
- Be mindful of seating. Power typically sits next to power. If you are the most senior person in the room, switch it up by sitting next to a junior team member. If you're more junior-level, show confidence by taking a seat beside the senior folks.
- Don't have the same meeting every time. Keep people fresh by mixing up formats and processes. Boredom is never interesting.

Speaking Engagements

Daily Grind Many professionals will at some point be asked to speak about a topic, whether as part of an industry panel (as I described earlier) or during a conference breakout session or a program with an audience of hundreds. At worst, speaking is a dreaded experience. More often, it's tolerated but falls to the bottom of the priority list in a person's busy work life. Slides are generally thrown together at the last minute. The most typical approach to content is to play it relatively safe and to come across as credible and professional. "Do no reputational harm" is the unconscious intention.

In speaking engagements, the audience is expecting to be inspired. It's a wide-open opportunity to shine.

Shining Moment Speaking in public provides a larger spotlight than any other situation described in this chapter. The audience is primed to be inspired and entertained and is surprised and delighted when that happens. Perhaps part of the expectation is that the speaker will be larger than life and come with unique insights and striking viewpoints that push us to think. It's a wide-open opportunity to shine.

- Again, start by setting your situational intention for the audience. Use the Intentionality Frame to structure your thoughts.
- Consider how you might use strategic shock value in your comments. Start off with a powerful statement that grabs people's

attention. State something counterintuitive or contradictory to conventional wisdom. One of my opening lines for CEO workshops is, "You already know most of what I have to say—but you don't do it." When I spoke to companies about how to get more PR, I sometimes opened with, "No one cares about you." It underscored my point that you must work hard for coverage in a crowded marketplace.

- Be bold in your delivery. Structure your talk to include statements that convey what the audience is thinking but might not say. At a venture capital conference in 2001, after the dot-com bust left investors wary of companies with plenty of "eyeballs" but no business model, I heard an arresting CEO pitch for funding that was themed around this statement: "We have actual customers. They pay us in real dollars." The speaker had credible information and delivered it in a tongue-in-cheek, deadpan style that brought lightness to an otherwise tough environment.

- Make your comments easy for people to follow. It's a basic lesson from public speaking 101: "Tell them what you're going to say, say it, then recap what you said." I like using lists (e.g., "Four imperatives for financial reform") to help the audience follow your points.

- If you're comfortable doing so, use humor. It relaxes people and is an engaging diversion. Tell jokes or share funny anecdotes. Not every humorous comment has to produce guffaws to be successful. Small amusements work, too. *Drive* author Dan Pink and I were both speakers at the Association for Financial Professionals conference in 2010, and I caught his session. He spoke to a group just after lunch, when people are notoriously tired, so he used it to his advantage. He opened by saying that he was a shrewd negotiator. When asked to speak he said sure, but on two conditions: "I must speak right after lunch and only in a room with absolutely no natural light."

- Practice your entire talk out loud to establish that all-important muscle memory. For stories and jokes especially, saying them out loud helps to establish their rhythm.

- If you're part of a panel, resist the urge to show agreement by reinforcing what other panelists have said. Instead, look for opportunities to put a new twist on others' points, or respectfully offer a counterpoint. For example, "Jane makes a great point, and I'd like to present another way of approaching it."

- Invite questions at the end, or even better, during your presentation. Realize that the audience comes first—not your content. Be flexible about adapting your presentation or shortening it to capture audience interaction.

Press Interviews

Daily Grind   Because of restrictive corporate policies around who talks to the press, few people find themselves in conversations with reporters. However, if you're the CEO or a functional leader, you may find yourself talking to reporters frequently. Many of the same factors encountered in speaking engagements are at play here; namely, people generally seek to play it safe and demonstrate expertise. During interviews, executives stick to their key points and anxiously avoid any unflattering topics. Practically no one enjoys media interviews because they are high-risk. A successful interview is one where you got all your points out and the reporter didn't ask tough questions you weren't prepared to answer.

Shining Moment   Reporters are people, too—even if we are slightly intimidated by their power. Being interesting works the same for reporters as it does for other audience members. Of course, you do have to take some extra care to communicate artfully and precisely with reporters (after all, your comments can wind up being read by millions of people). Accuracy is your first goal. However, the more engaging you are in your communications, the more reporters will come back to you for more interviews.

> *Reporters are people, too. They respond as any other audience does. Be interesting, but also be exceedingly accurate.*

- Start any interview by asking the reporter what he needs to get out of the interview and what the news outlet's readership would find helpful. Don't make it all about you.
- Come prepared with short sound bites for talking points, intriguing stories and anecdotes, and telling statistics. When you get a chance to talk, be interesting to listen to.

- Know the latest news affecting your industry and be ready to comment about it. Again, as much as reasonably possible, take a bold stand: Question an industry practice, make a prediction, or counter conventional wisdom.
- Use declarations here too. Be direct in your responses. Be aware of and avoid saying "I think" and "We might."
- Avoid rambling while answering. Not only does it play into a common reporter tactic for getting uncensored comments, but droning also makes you less interesting as an interviewee. Remember, no one cares about the topic as much as you do. Get to your point and then stop.
- Show excitement and enthusiasm. An interview shouldn't feel like a lie detector test. Smile (even if you are on the phone) and bring your personality into the conversation.

Sales and Client Meetings

Daily Grind   While only some professionals speak in public or to the press, just about everybody meets with clients and potential clients. Most of the time, sales and client meetings are content driven and focused on getting the audience to like/respect/pay us. Demonstrating credibility is paramount. PowerPoint is the weapon of choice.

Shining Moment   The most common presumption in sales and client meetings is that the presenters are there to inform the audience. The onus is on you, as the presenter. The audience may have its guard up, especially in sales situations. Therefore, one of the best ways to be more engaging in these meetings goes back to the trust equation. When you focus on building trust, you also increase your presence, your likability, and your credibility. You also come across as refreshingly different, interesting, and memorable. Revisit Chapter 6 for ideas around building trust in "Situations Where Trust Is Hard to Come By" (including selling) and how to apply the trust equation to sales meetings. In addition, here are other ideas to try.

When meeting with clients and prospects, focus on trust first.

- Set your situational intention ahead of time. (Sounds like a broken record, I know, but it works!)

- Be personable and real. Shed the all-business persona and share stories about yourself. While people are filing into the room and you are waiting for everyone to assemble, it's a perfect time for casual connection.
- Be conscientious of people's time, just like in internal meetings. Ask what your clients or prospects need first, and don't assume your presentation will answer all their questions. Never put your content above your audience's questions. Don't appear frustrated to be taken off topic.
- Show integrity. Don't be afraid to admit when you don't have an answer or that a project has been difficult or that a product or service has a weakness. At a time when so much of corporate life is about CYA, honesty stands out. I love the expression "Put some skunk on the table." It's the idea that in sales, you draw your prospect closer by admitting a product or service's weaknesses, instead of just highlighting the strengths.
- Put the relationship above all else. Focus on how to be of service to the other person, even if that means you'll miss out on something this time around. I feel like a part-time recruiter for all the people I've matched up with jobs over the years. Generally, I'm acting in service to clients or colleagues who have an open position for which I can help find a good candidate. I also make introductions that can lead to sales, partnerships, or coaching relationships. I readily refer people to others if I'm not the best fit. Relationships develop over the long term. And what comes around goes around.

Discomfort Is as Natural as the Spotlight Itself

Being in the spotlight causes a unique sense of natural discomfort. We've been told our whole lives to be team players. We're rewarded for "taking one for the team." Culturally, we abhor show-offs and have plenty of pejorative terms to describe them. Sitting quietly in the back and biding our time has been instilled in us as a good and honorable approach.

All that is true, and as a leader, there are times when the very best thing you can do for the team is to take the stage. And when you get there, the most altruistic move you can make is to play as big as you can. We want our leaders to engage and inspire. We expect them to be a little different. We like them to be *good interesting*. So, bring it on!

Key Takeaways from Chapter 12

1. While many leaders bristle at being in the spotlight, people expect it. It's not about personal ego but about accepting the role and learning to play on a bigger stage.
2. Part of being inspiring is simply being interesting. Having a point of view on a wide range of industry issues, telling relatable stories, and making bold statements allow you to use the leadership stage to bring more attention to your company.
3. There's *good interesting* and then there's *bad interesting*. We all know what bad interesting is: grandstanding, being confrontational, having the last word, and hogging the limelight. It's important to stay away from being interesting in the bad way, but there's a big difference between acting like that and drawing positive attention to oneself.
4. Every executive's workday offers multiple opportunities to inspire. There are networking events, team meetings, speaking engagements, or client meetings to attend. When we aren't intentional about using these opportunities as spotlight moments, we miss out on a chance to establish leadership presence.
5. As a leader, when you accept that the spotlight is not in addition to your regular job but a core part of it, then you have a different problem to solve. If you have the spotlight regardless, what are you going to do with it? How do you maximize it for good?

Ideas I Want to Try from Chapter 12:

_____

_____

_____

_____

_____

CHAPTER 13

Bringing It All Together: Presence in a Pinch

So here we are at the conclusion of the book. And here you are, ready for an important meeting where you'll be presenting your ideas about a new program at your company. You want to come across at your most compelling, confident, and authentic best.

How can you condense 200+ pages of ideas from this book into the 30 minutes you've set aside for preparation for your next meeting or event? I've got you covered. This chapter is for you.

As we head toward the finish line, let's reflect back on the three-step I-Presence model: intentional, individual, and inspirational. Did you notice that the model moves from inward to outward? That's exactly how presence works. It starts with you, builds through your connection to others, and ultimately catalyzes through your communications. Each piece is important on its own, and it is the combination that catapults leaders to a new level.

As we have learned from neuroscience, if people don't act on new learning quickly and in workable increments, it is far less likely that they'll achieve sustained behavior change. I want to keep these concepts alive for you so that even during the most stressful day, when you are focused on a dozen action items, you can show your strongest and best presence as you lead and inspire others.

So, in this wrap-up chapter, I'm creating "crib notes" that provide a quick recap of salient points from the book. Use this chapter as an ongoing reference guide—what I call the *I-Presence Prep Guide*—an in-the-moment overview that you can come back to before your next big meeting, presentation, or important conversation. At the end of the chapter, I've also included a brief questionnaire that may be helpful as a "presence practice sheet." Now, let's go through each element of the Prep Guide (see Figure 13-1) as a reminder.

Intention
Personal brand
Situational intention
Full-body practice
Pregame ritual

Physicality
Posture
Movement
Facial expressions
Voice

Connection
Understanding
Trust
Listening
Acknowledgment

Language
↑ Reward ↓ Threat
Declarations
Stories
Daring

Figure 13-1.   I-Presence Prep Guide.

Prepare with Intention

Whether you have 30 minutes or 30 days to prepare, always start with intention. Everything flows from it. Consider intention your strategy, or the part you can most easily affect ahead of time so that you'll have less to worry about during your event. Spend time preparing with intention and you'll be more likely to stave off anxiety, distracting body language, lack of clarity, and other factors that can derail your presence. You may think this is the easiest part to skip when you are pressed for time. But it's actually the most critical.

Personal Presence Brand. Your personal presence brand is what you want to be known for in general terms. It is the image that's readily connected to you when people mention your name, whether inside or outside the company. A personal presence brand is relatively static and underscores your values and aspirations. You should be able to condense your brand down to just two or three words (e.g., "motivating and visionary," "credible, caring catalyst," or "change agent") and carry it with you at all times. All intentions and the majority of your actions should enhance your personal brand, not detract from it. In this way, it becomes a personal guide for making decisions about what you say, where you go, and what you'll do when you get there.

Situational Intention. This is like a swing thought—the last thing that goes through your mind as you hit the golf ball off the tee. Your situational intention is what you want to impart in a particular event that is unique to the situation. Here's a simple way to consider it: As people leave your presentation, what do you want to hear them chattering about? Remember that humans process information on emotional terms. So whatever you want people to feel, you must first embody. If you'd like the reaction to be "excited and optimistic," then you need to display those very qualities. "Excited and optimistic" therefore becomes your situational intention. (To map your main talking points to your situational intention, use the Intentionality Frame, as described in Chapter 1.)

Full-Body Practice. When we are relaxed, there's a natural alignment between our minds and our bodies. We can sense a misalignment when we stop to take notice. Practice by simulating the actual event as much as possible. Say your thoughts out loud while either standing or sitting; in other words, practice the way you'll be making your presentation. In this manner, you create muscle memory for your words and your body language. When you're in the moment and anxiety kicks in, you'll have a frame of reference that will make the experience more intuitive. If you don't have time to practice your full presentation out loud, rehearse your opening remarks and the major points you need to make.

Pregame Ritual. A pregame ritual gets you in the zone for your event. It's meant to stimulate the feelings you need to embody, allay nerves, and keep you focused. Everyone's pregame rituals are different: Try cranking up a favorite song or joking with a friend, or practice deep breathing or even quiet contemplation of your intention. It doesn't matter what your ritual is. Just find one that works and make it a repeatable practice.

Align Your Physicality to Your Intention

Hopefully you've rehearsed and have a strong sense of how you want to appear when you take the stage (literally or otherwise). Remember the three-part body check: face, gestures, and posture. Try to sense alignment with your intention in each of these domains as you go, and tweak them as needed. Don't worry about perfect form. Instead, focus on what felt right to you naturally, in your relaxed state. And keep in mind that impressions are built over time—even if that time is only 15 minutes! A few distracting movements will not curtail an otherwise effective presentation. Chances are you'll notice more of your missteps than anyone else will.

Posture. It is the first aspect of body language that we notice. That's why we want to scream at the slumped-over teenager, "Straighten up!" For any executive, posture should be strong, with shoulders back and head up. Whether sitting or standing, notice if your stance is open or closed. Unless your intention is to ward off an unscrupulous salesperson, then your arms should be open with both feet planted on the ground. Be mindful of a common posture default: closed arms and crossed legs. Even when its purpose is to conserve heat in an overly air-conditioned office, this posture communicates defensiveness.

Movement. Any movement or gesture that you normally make is fine as long as it does not distract from your intention. As you practiced, you may have developed assured gestures to emphasize certain points. Perhaps you walked around to keep energy up. Repeat that movement in your presentation. When I'm speaking, I like to come out from behind the podium and even go into the audience to increase my connection to others. Yet for some people, that may not feel natural and could increase nervousness. If that's the case, don't worry about it. Instead, use your body check to avoid distracting, unintentional gestures such as toying with a pen, playing with your hair, or gripping the podium for dear life.

Facial Expressions. Nearly all professionals need to smile more. It's the easiest way to have a more gracious, approachable presence. Body language and mood have a circular effect, so not only does a positive intention create positive body language, but the reverse is true as well. Smiling helps to solidify a positive intention. Unless the situation you are addressing is grave, remember to smile. If you can't remember, write reminders in your notes.

Voice. Strong leaders speak with certainty and confidence. The tone of your voice creates perception. Tape-record yourself while you are talking and then replay it to gain valuable insight on how you sound to others. Speaking in declarative terms—"We will," not "We might"—shows a self-assured presence. Caveats are not inspiring. Also, learn to be comfortable with pauses. First, pausing is quite natural for listeners because it allows them to get ready for your next point. Second, a pause allows a speaker time to collect his thoughts. It's fine even to pause and lose track for a second, as long as you come back strong. (Others won't know if it was intentional or not.)

Find the Connection Points

Whether your audience is one person or 1,000, their acceptance of you is largely based on their connection to you. In those presence-defining moments when we need to present ourselves, it's common to focus on being perfect. We spend most of our energy developing the perfect words that we try to communicate in the perfect way. There's certainly a level of competence and clarity to meet, but it's just one part of how others assess your presence. Perfection can be alienating. Connection is about finding the humanity in others. If you want to strengthen your presence, consider how to foster trust and empathy. For many of us, this requires attention and deliberation.

Understanding. Understanding is a major piece of empathy—one that starts before you even enter the meeting room. Know your audience. Before you present, find out what their concerns are and if there is any relevant history. With small audiences, learn about their personal backgrounds. The more valid information you have, the more you'll be able to address the concerns in the room. Go into a conversation assuming you don't have all the information and seek out others' perspectives. This can be an effective way to connect with even a large audience. Tell them what you understand about their situation, and then ask for their comments, which should provide greater detail.

Trust. Trust is foundational to presence. Your communications will not get through as intended unless you can establish trust. Human beings constantly assess one another as "friend or foe." When trust is absent, we place the other person squarely in the foe category. We literally process a foe's words in a different part of our brains than we do a friend's! As you recall from Chapter 6, the components of the trust equation are credibility, reliability, intimacy, and self-orientation. As you prepare your comments, consider how you are touching on each of these components and building trust.

Listening. While listening sounds obvious and easy, it's often absent when it counts the most. One of the best ways to increase connection is to become a great listener. Focus on the person in front of you, ask open-ended questions, clarify and rephrase, and curtail your own opinion. Whether it's during an open Q&A or behind a closed door, true listening conveys empathy to the other person, and as a nice by-product, you may just learn something new.

Acknowledgment. Workplace presentations, especially those involving new ideas and change, can become tense with so much at personal stake for the players. Acknowledgment is one way to keep everyone on the same side of the table. It's the ability to say "I can see your position," even if you don't agree with it. It boosts empathy and changes the interpersonal dynamic. It strengthens your presence because it shows confidence in remaining open to opposing viewpoints. Much of a leader's work is gaining buy-in, which requires others to feel heard and considered.

Use Language to Inspire

Leaders need to inspire and motivate to create followership. A core part of a leader's job is to cultivate change on individual and broad scales. The study of neuroscience teaches us about the fundamental human reluctance to change and how to overcome it by helping people form ideas, focus on solutions, and act on moments of insight. Setting a compelling vision through language is a key part of managing change. Even the best vision is meaningless if it can't be communicated and received clearly.

Increasing Rewards/Minimizing Threats. When presenting any information that hints of change, you'll have the best reception if you consider the universal triggers that cause defensive reactions in others: threats to status, certainty, autonomy, and fairness. As much as possible, assure people on each of these fronts.

Declarations. Declarations are bold, assured statements that attract energy. They open up new possibilities. In a corporate world dominated by CYA behavior, when you make clear declarations—"I/We *will* do X"—people sit up and take notice. Successful leaders use declarations to move people, create excitement, show courage, illuminate a company's raison d'être, and invoke change. Incorporate them where you can. And remember, if you fall short, be accountable; use the opportunity to learn and keep moving forward.

Stories. The human brain has evolved to process stories efficiently. That's because for much of our time on the planet, stories provided vital information for our very survival. We enjoy telling and hearing stories. So, find ways to bring your own stories into your communications. Stories help people to know you and understand your values—and that increases trust. Stories are memorable. They aid in understanding complex concepts. And you are your most authentic when you are telling a story. The best stories are to the point, contain common reference points, and show struggle and achievement.

Daring. Part of a compelling presence is being interesting. As a leader, you are often in the spotlight, so it benefits everyone if you learn to play on a bigger stage. Be a visionary by cultivating an aspirational vision that's personal to you, and share it actively. Dare to divulge opinions, bold stories, or a controversial stance on an issue. When you have to present, contemplate how to be different rather than one of the pack. Having a presence with a bit of shock value can be a good strategy.

Ready to Bring Your Best Self

At the beginning of this book, I discussed how much interest executive presence generates in companies today. Yet paradoxically, it's difficult for the average professional to focus on it. Presence does seem personal, nebulous, and hard to execute. My hope is that I've taken some squishy concepts and helped them to take shape for you. I want you to be excited about your own ability to affect your presence in a way that will make your goals imminently achievable. In fact, it's not all that hard. It just takes focus. Use the questionnaire in Figure 13-2 as a "practice sheet" for focusing on your own I-Presence.

Remember, as you head into that all-important meeting, you already have every ounce of presence you need in various parts of your life. All you are doing is integrating them to present your best self—your strongest presence—more purposefully and frequently. Don't try to be perfect. It's not about using every best practice you've ever learned or reshaping your personality.

Set an intention, go with what's authentic for you, and wow them.

Wish I could be there.

⊖ Presence™
Prep Sheet

⊖ntentional

My overarching personal presence brand is:	
I want people to leave this discussion feeling:	
To support this intention, the emotion I want to exhibit is:	
I will create dissonance if I fall into this habit or pattern:	

⊖ndividual

The motivation of this person/group is: *(If I don't know, how will I get it?)*	
The relationship to his/her/their overall objectives is:	
I will listen and acknowledge their perspective by:	
I will share this about myself:	
I will increase trust by:	

⊖nspirational

My pregame ritual to embody my intention is:	
How will I address the groups' "What's in It for Me"?	
The stories, examples, and quotes I will use to support my points are:	
I will practice these critical points out loud:	
My body language must be: (i.e., posture, movement, eye contact, facial expression, tone)	
My key declarations and interesting points will be:	

Figure 13-2. I-Presence practice sheet.

CHAPTER 14

Afterword

In the middle of writing this book, I was digging through old files and came across notes I had written to myself. The notes were an effort to process some leadership issues I was facing at the time. This was in the same period that I mentioned at the start of the book, when I felt as though everyone wanted a piece of me and I was driving full throttle and simultaneously building the car. Filled with frustration, the words were hard to read. I wanted to reach through time and give myself a come-to-Jesus shake to say, "Give yourself a break! Enough with the self-flagellation! Just do this, this, and this—and it will be fine." But of course, 15 years' worth of learning takes, well, fifteen years. I had to earn this hindsight. I have a sneaking suspicion that a few years from now I'll have a similar experience about something I've done more recently. And so it goes.

Presence is ever elusive. Beware of people who claim they've got it all figured out. It's a work in progress, a jumping-off point, the residue from a lifetime comedy of errors. Improving our presence takes humility, faith, courage, and a healthy sense of humor. We are all learners at this party. I hope I've created a book that shows you where I am: right beside you, and learning all the time.

In fact, presence is underscored by a confident commitment to openness and learning. As the proverb goes, when the student is ready the teacher appears. Now that you have embarked on this journey, you'll see mentors everywhere you look. You'll find yourself observing others differently, with a new set of distinctions about what makes someone else charismatic or motivating—or neither. This act alone will help you strengthen your presence. You'll not only apply concepts from the book, but you'll see how others use them in real time.

Presence must be carefully balanced with a strong sense of who you are at your core—your authentic self. When we try to be everything to everyone, our presence is like a reed in the wind. When we try to do everything, we face exhaustion and risk a mental shutdown. It's vital to pick the parts of presence that you can leverage, the parts that excite and inspire you to do better and be more. A strong presence is, after all, the best version of you.

One of the aspects of coaching that I love most is bearing witness to other people's truest selves, when they are most authentic, real, and engaging. Coaching isn't an environment where it pays to hold back. Clients discard the subterfuge and present raw issues right beside their own pent-up emotions about solving them. Together we create a mix of new thoughts and behaviors. I see presence at its purest and fullest, and then I hold my breath, hoping that the other person can keep it out in front, when professional life has a thick mask right outside our door just begging to be worn. After all, the connection and trust found in a coaching relationship are rare in the workplace. But just imagine what would happen if they were pervasive.

After working with top leaders for the past couple decades, I am often referred to as an executive communications expert. I've worked hard to build a reputation for making executives more successful, and I've been honored to apply my ideas and skills to benefit others— many in positions of considerable influence. I've had to be vigilantly intentional about role modeling a presence that's confident, unflappable, and poised, or I wouldn't have been able to build a profitable business. Readers who have worked with me may be surprised at the behind-the-scenes stories. The fact is, I'm not a presence expert; I'm an expert presence learner. I'm continuously gaining new insights and applying them. It's interesting how these presence concepts work in an ongoing virtuous cycle. As I wrote the book, I once again had to use the very same tenets of I-Presence: to be intentional about writing an accessible book, to build individual connection through trust and empathy, and to inspire through a vision and clear communications. I hope I succeeded.

Since I first made a declaration in January 2010 that I was going to document my experiences with executive presence, there have been more moments than I could count when someone has asked me for a resource such as this book. The struggle that professionals face to better themselves in this area shows no signs of abating. To me, this is a good direction for leadership. Executive presence is the corporate "it" factor for a reason: We need to be stewards of our organizations and to win over hearts and minds rather than take them for granted or consider them as afterthoughts.

Whenever I hear someone say, "My boss suggested I work on my executive presence," I also hear the subtext, "It's recognized in my organization that presence is important and can be learned." Leaders who choose to focus on their presence are sending an indelible message that connection is the path to greatness. When you inspire and motivate, your influence creates a self-perpetuating cycle of new possibilities for others. Who knows where it ends? We're all fortunate to be part of it, even if in a small way.

I wish you the best of luck, and excitement and reward, as you go forward from here. While presence itself is open to interpretation, here are a few pieces of advice I know for sure will help you on your path to strengthening it.

Pay attention. The simple act of noticing your own behavior and that of others, in a deeper way, will create an ongoing focal point on presence. When someone inspires you (or fails to), take a moment to understand why.

Maintain a sense of humor. Learn from your mistakes, and learn to laugh at them, too. Remember, things are rarely as bad (or as good) as you think they are.

Be brave. It's hard to extend yourself by trying new behaviors, especially when failure can mean public embarrassment. Summon the courage to be uncomfortable. You won't get anywhere by playing it safe. Put yourself out there.

Go easy on yourself. No one is perfect, and yes, that includes you. You'll notice 90 percent more of your mess-ups than anyone else will. Smile, and keep going.

Don't get hung up on doing the right anything. What works for one person can bomb for someone else. Presence is your personal essence; it's a unique composite of behaviors. You'll encounter many people who will tell you that you must do it their way. Keep an open mind. But if it feels foreign to you after trying it a few times, skip it.

When all else fails, walk tall, keep your head up, and look people in the eye. In nearly every aspect of our lives, my grandmother's advice endures.

Kristi Hedges

Acknowledgments

Writing this book has been a dream of mine for a long time, and I'm still pinching myself that my dream is now a reality. A heartfelt thanks to all the friends who helped me along in this process by providing encouragement, wisdom, introductions, and ideas.

Thanks to my rock-star agent Molly Lyons, who loved my proposal at first sight and took me on as a client. Without her, it would still be an idea sitting in the back of my head. Thanks as well to Ellen Kadin, Louis Greenstein, Jim Bessent, Barry Richardson, and the AMACOM team for giving the book the perfect home and for strengthening the message.

Thanks to all of my clients and colleagues who I've been honored to work with. You've taught me more than you know. While you are anonymous in these pages, you are real in my heart. Thanks to the wonderful coaching community at Georgetown for first introducing me to the ideas of inner presence and intention. It's been life-changing. Thanks to my Element North business partner, Mike McGinley, for his spot-on feedback and ridiculous amount of faith in me.

Thanks to my early draft readers, Chris Segall and Mary Knebel, who were way too busy but found time anyway. Your comments made a world of difference. Thanks to my Vistage chair, Clyde Northrop, for some of the best advice of my life.

Thanks to the folks who were kind enough to be interviewed or to grant permission to use their material in this book, including David Rock, Dan Pink, Charles H. Green, Ted Leonsis, Niki Leondakis,

Chalmers Brothers, Scott Eblin, Greg Stock, Jim Kaitz, and Michael Dering. Your words made the book so much stronger.

Thanks to Virginia Tech professors Rachel Holloway and Bob Denton for first getting me passionate about communications as a social science, and for investing so much time and advice all those years ago in an ambitious (if typically distracted) college kid. Go Hokies!

Finally, the deepest thanks go to my entire family for their constant love, support, and unfailing belief in me, and to my late grandmothers for enduring inspiration. To the two best kids in the world, Smith and Emery, who were so patient with an already-busy mother who seemed to be forever writing. I'm so proud to be your mom. And for my husband, Mike, who was in this, as in all things, the consummate friend, supporter, adviser, and champion. You make everything good.

Appendix:
Quick Hit I-Presence Tips

"What Should I Keep Top of Mind if I'm a _____":
General Considerations for Specific Situations

On these pages you'll find checklists of the most common presence considerations and topline suggestions for CEOs and senior leaders, entrepreneurs, women, job seekers, career changers, and young professionals. Each checklist is arranged by the three I-Presence elements: intentional, individual, and inspirational. Think of these pages as a resource to spur ideas, frame the I-Presence concepts in the book, and help you assess where you stand compared to others in similar situations.

Ultimately, it's your authentic presence, and it's up to you to decide what works.

PRESENCE CONSIDERATIONS FOR CEOs AND SENIOR LEADERS

If you are a CEO or senior leader, you've already exhibited a great amount of presence to get to your current job. The challenge now is how to leverage your expertise and functional competency into a more inspiring and motivating leadership role. (Hence Marshall Goldsmith's adage "What got you here won't get you there.") Having an inspirational executive presence means having the right touch—not too hard nor too soft, yet always accountable. There's also more pressure to be in the spotlight and to fully capitalize on your position.

Part 1: Intentional

✔ Candid feedback can be hard for leaders to obtain; yet you need it now more than ever. Conduct your personal presence audit to determine your strengths, then use those strengths to develop a clear personal presence brand. Select trusted associates for quick feedback points (QFPs) so that the data keeps coming.

✔ Actively use situational intentions to inject emotional resonance into communications with critical audiences (including your team members). Set the tone intentionally; don't allow it to happen by accident.

✔ When you have important information to communicate, take the time to practice out loud with your full body. Because people scrutinize their leaders' actions for implicit signs, misaligned body language can lead to serious static in your messages. Remember, you carry a red blinking light that screams *this is important*.

Part 2: Individual

✔ You've racked up numerous accomplishments to get to your position. You're the go-to person with the right answers. But these qualities can intimidate those around you. So let people get to know you by sharing some of your personal interests, triumphs, and struggles. Be transparent about your thinking so people know how you approach situations.

✔ Leaders need to constantly gauge and build trust or they won't be successful. Senior leaders often have the credibility and reliability pieces down pat. To strengthen trust, concentrate on building intimacy and lowering your own self-orientation.

✔ Have a deep understanding of what motivates your direct reports and as many others in your organization as you can. When new hires come on board, take them to lunch first thing and spend the time uncovering what they truly want to accomplish for themselves and how this job can help them get it.

Part 3: Inspirational

✔ A big part of your job is managing constant change, so remember the lessons of neuroscience and David Rock's SCARF model (as covered in Chapter 9). If you want to temper defensive reactions, support people's need for status, certainty, autonomy, relatedness, and fairness. Weave this approach into your everyday communications.

✔ Set a vision that creates a strong sense of purpose for your team that rises above any financial or market goals. The vision can support corporate goals, but it should also be meaningful on its own. Make it aspirational and personal. And ensure the vision is shared and active.

✔ Once you get the big title you'll notice that lots more eyes are on you. Don't shirk from the attention—step into the spotlight. Be daring, bold, interesting, and real. It's no longer in anyone's interest for you to remain safely in the background.

PRESENCE CONSIDERATIONS FOR ENTREPRENEURS

An entrepreneur's situation is similar to a CEO's or a senior leader's with one exception: Many entrepreneurs step into their positions suddenly, rather than rising through the ranks. There's scant time for acclimation. Entrepreneurial companies generally move faster, make constant course corrections, and have less structure and process than established companies. It's a wild ride for everyone involved, including the leader. Entrepreneurs are known for their passion, slavish commitment, and personal investment. In a supercharged entrepreneurial environment, executive presence can be an afterthought rather than what it truly is—a key means of achieving success.

Part 1: Intentional

✔ You're the window into your company. Whatever your presence conveys will be attributed to the entire organization. Set an intention for your personal presence brand that embodies the characteristics you'd like for your company (e.g., innovative, reliable, customer-focused).

✔ An entrepreneur's passion can cause her to neglect what's important to the audience during meetings and other interactions or exchanges. Use the Intentionality Frame (found in Chapter 1) to keep your points crisp and relevant.

✔ With the rate of change in emerging companies, entrepreneurs need to be a magnet for feedback. Set a culture in your company where everyone speaks the truth—including to you—and reward them for it. Institute quick feedback points (QFPs) and start by asking for QFPs from someone a few levels down from you.

Part 2: Individual

✔ Connecting takes time, and time is the entrepreneur's enemy. Even if you're still in the trenches with your team, set aside specific times to catch up. Schedule weekly one-on-ones with your direct reports and reach out to next-level downs on a regular basis, just to check in. Seek to know two or three things you have in common with as many others in your company as possible.

✔ Entrepreneurial companies run on trust. (In fact, at some entrepreneurial companies, trust is all there is.) As the company grows, find ways to keep people informed about what's going right and how you are handling failures. Your self-orientation will be assumed to be high. After all, it's your baby. Take strategic moments to show how you are acting in other people's best interests, not just your own.

✔ Nowadays, it can be all too easy to rely on email to manage employees. Be mindful not to delegate tasks via email that would be better discussed in person, and never use email to send negative feedback. If in doubt, save the email and revisit it in the morning before sending.

Part 3: Inspirational

✔ Entrepreneurs have the opportunity to set a clear and guiding purpose, and to create a vision that means something to people. Because start-up companies can't always afford to pay large salaries, a sense of purpose can motivate and help you retain excellent employees. Don't waste this advantage. Take the time to figure out what your vision is. Make the vision aspirational, personal, shared, and active.

✔ Entrepreneurial companies create greenfield opportunities where people can do their best work with few restrictions. It's the perfect confluence of events to enable flow, whereby people bring their full attention and skills to bear. However, a constant threat of uncertainty can undermine this process. Be vigilant about conveying information and helping people to see why their work will transcend any future events to positively impact their careers and potentially their larger world.

✔ Readily adopt the notion of yourself as a thought-leader and throw yourself into the conversation in your marketplace. Be a go-to source on your industry, taking every opportunity to speak to groups or to engage in traditional and social media. Dare to be interesting and provocative. Attention drawn to you goes straight to your company.

PRESENCE CONSIDERATIONS FOR WOMEN

I'm frequently asked to comment on specific presence considerations for women, which is challenging because women's situations are so varied. We are not a monolithic group with universally shared issues. That said, I concede that there are certain characteristics given to women (and often adopted by us as well) that can make presence an extra struggle. Stereotypes and cautionary tales abound for executive women. How many times have we heard the dichotomy that if a woman is too tough, she's a bitch, and if she's too soft, she's not up to the job? For women, the boundaries can seem confining and narrow. Luckily, the steps to a strong presence help expand both thoughts and options.

Part 1: Intentional

✔ Conduct a personal presence audit to get an accurate picture of how you are perceived. Women can be extremely hard on themselves, so the more external data the better.

✔ Uncover any negative intentions that may be getting in your way. Challenge them by turning pessimistic thoughts into optimistic ones.

✔ Set a bold personal presence intention. As you develop it, consider the qualities of both female and male leaders who have had an effect on you.

Part 2: Individual

✔ Women can be highly susceptible to perfectionism. Aim for excellence, not perfection. Actively find ways to communicate your own struggles, and how you've overcome them, to use as examples for others.

✔ Make sure that you are focusing on the various aspects of trust—credibility, reliability, intimacy, and low self-orientation. Women have a lower threshold for bragging, which can cause them to hold back their accomplishments and lose out on chances to enhance credibility.

✔ While many would argue that women are better at expressing empathy and connecting than men, statistically, they have less time at the office to do it. According to the 2009 "American Time Use Study" from the U.S. Bureau of Labor Statistics, women work 45 minutes less per day than male full-time workers. The gap is attributed to women spending more time doing most household responsibilities.[1] Collegial catch-up often occurs around the workday fringes—precisely when women often find they are pinched for time. It's critical to make those connections, so find ways to incorporate touch points into your day. Schedule lunches and coffees. Practice management by walking around.

Part 3: Inspirational

✔ Women are often described as natural collaborators. That's a good thing, but it can prevent us from stepping out front. Take the time to set a vision for yourself and/or your team. It's not about ego. Vision requires bold strokes.

✔ Make strong declarations about what you *will* do. Take every opportunity to demonstrate how you are achieving your declarations to create excitement and a sense of purpose. Avoid hedging. It waters down your power.

✔ Women have the same opportunity as men to be daring, witty, and even skillfully light. Yet, at times, we can oversteer into seriousness in an effort to demonstrate strength and competency. Remember to balance competency with vulnerability. Think of how you communicate with your friends and bring that authentic self into the workplace. Express more, not less. Excitement is contagious.

PRESENCE CONSIDERATIONS FOR JOB SEEKERS

Whether you are looking for your first job or your last one, your executive presence will carry more weight than anything else once you make it to the interview stage. (And with senior executives, that usually starts well before any formal job search process, through your interactions in your network and in business settings.)

Part 1: Intentional

✔ Be crystal clear about your personal presence brand before you begin job seeking. Know what you want to demonstrate through your words and actions.

✔ Use the Intentionality Frame to configure your main points for interviews.

✔ Practice key points about yourself and your experience out loud. Take careful note of your body language to ensure it is in alignment with your intention. Make sure you smile often.

Part 2: Individual

✔ Come up with three or four stories about your life and experience that communicate your values, achievements, struggles, and passion. Keep them handy for formal or informal interviews, to let others see the authentic you. As an extra bonus, stories make you more memorable.

✔ Trust is the name of the game in hiring. Someone has to trust that the chance he is taking on you is a good bet. Review the section "Getting Hired" in Chapter 6 for how to embolden trust.

✔ Find commonalities with each person that you meet, either before or during the interview process.

Part 3: Inspirational

✔ Have a vision for the domain you are seeking to lead—whether it's a sole-contributor position, a team, or the whole company. Walk in the door ready to share the possibilities you see.

✔ Use inspired language. Make declarations about what you *will* do (not could or might do) if you get hired.

✔ Share opinions about common topics (i.e., show you are *good interesting*) and reveal sincere struggles as well. Be human, authentic, and real.

PRESENCE CONSIDERATIONS FOR CAREER CHANGERS

From baby boomers redefining themselves in retirement to market forces changing entire industries overnight, more people are changing careers than ever before. It can be simultaneously thrilling and scary to shift your identity after working so hard to establish yourself in a career. All of a sudden your solid ground feels shaky, and you end up dealing with feelings you hadn't faced in years. But here's the rub: Your ability to make this shift successfully is directly related to your ability to demonstrate a strong presence while doing it. If you want others to trust your capabilities in your newfound career, you have to comport yourself in a way that shows *you* believe you can do it.

Part 1: Intentional

✔ Accept the fact that your new life will require a new set of intentions. Whatever brand you had before might not be relevant now. As you get to know people in your new field, solicit their feedback for a personal presence audit. Their feedback will give you the most relevant information for how you'll need to "show up" (i.e., what you need to be a player) in this new world.

✔ Set intentions for all your interactions with others, from networking events to interviews. Get yourself in the zone beforehand with a pregame ritual.

✔ Gather success stories (even if they are carryovers from your last profession) to show what makes you excited about this new work. Carefully note your body language to keep it open and assured. Smile readily. Practice your points out loud and be sure not to come across as apologetic.

Part 2: Individual

✔ Don't forget the path that got you here. As you present yourself at interviews or networking events, share how your past has informed your present and how it prepared you for this new endeavor. It's what makes you unique.

✔ As with any hiring situation, you need to establish trust quickly. Show why you are credible and reliable for *this* career by providing similar examples from your past career.

✔ Resist the urge to put on the hard sell in an effort to overcompensate. Listen more than you talk. Acknowledge the concerns an interviewer may have about accepting you in this new role. Then show how you plan to overcome any obstacles the interviewer has described.

Part 3: Inspirational

✔ Energy goes a long way. When you tackle a new challenge you bring enthusiasm buttressed by a fresh perspective. Share your vision for what's possible for you in this new career. Don't be reticent. Be candid, and go as big as you can.

✔ Make compelling declarations about what you *will* do. Don't be hesitant.

✔ You have an interesting take on your new career simply because you come at it from a unique angle. Use this to your advantage. Be a thought-leader in the industry. Get involved in professional associations and peer groups. Create shining moments by being interesting.

PRESENCE CONSIDERATIONS FOR YOUNG PROFESSIONALS

Fledgling professionals can find it daunting to display a confident and credible presence while learning the ropes. When you are new to the workforce, you may lack role models for how to carry yourself in various situations. Rising professionals who exhibit an executive presence—way before ever being in an executive position—get swept into a virtuous cycle of perception. Young professionals who show leadership potential get noticed for it and end up with more opportunities to develop into leaders.

Part 1: Intentional

✔ Think of the leaders who have been meaningful to you—both in your work and private life. Write down their characteristics and make a short list of what you'd like to model, then begin developing a personal presence brand.

✔ Have a situational intention for every meeting you are in. Always contribute in some fashion. If you have nothing to add, ask an insightful question. Get there early enough to make small talk with others beforehand, and stay a few minutes after to do the same.

✔ Nervousness or insecurity can set in quickly, especially when so much is new. Focus on what you can control, such as your posture, facial expressions, and professional attire. Practice key points you want to make so they come across strong.

Part 2: Individual

✔ Be professional first, and bring the best parts of your personal life into the workplace. Think of some key stories that show what you're made of and find ways to communicate them. Overcame major obstacles to make your college soccer team? Perfect.

✔ When you are new in your career, people will look to see if you're credible and reliable enough to be trusted. Always do what you say you're going to do. If you are going to miss a deadline, communicate it well ahead of time. Be someone who can be counted on and good things will open up for you.

✔ Treat everyone, no matter the person's position or level of power, as a respected colleague. Be conversational, find commonalities, and bring up outside interests. Even the top guns at the office like to discuss their families and hobbies. Go to office happy hours with the goal of finding common interests with others, not to party on the company's dime.

Part 3: Inspirational

✔ Communicate a vision for your position. You don't want to come across as self-serving, so be sure that your vision benefits the company. Follow your industry, conduct informational interviews of experts, and read extensively. As you develop thoughts about what's happening in your market longer term, share them.

✔ Speak professionally and declaratively. Tape-record yourself to see if you have lingering college speak. Avoid using words such as "like" as an interjection (e.g., "I'm, like, serious . . . ") or saying "I think," which make you sound inexperienced and tentative. Aim to speak with conviction using a strong tone.

✔ Volunteer for opportunities that put you in a position of being noticed. If nothing comes your way, take an idea directly to your boss: Propose writing a research report, giving a presentation to colleagues about a topic you know well, or organizing a workplace cultural initiative (another reason it helps to stay up on the industry). The extra effort sets you apart and gives you a chance to shine.

Notes

Chapter 1: What Are You Thinking?

1. Jim Loehr and Tony Schwartz, "The Making of a Corporate Athlete," *Harvard Business Review,* January 2001, pp. 120–128.
2. Scott Eblin, *The Next Level: What Insiders Know About Executive Success* (Boston: Davies-Black, 2006).

Chapter 2: Your Actions Are Speaking So Loudly I Can Hardly Hear What You're Saying

1. Albert Mehrabian, *Silent Messages: Implicit Communication of Emotions and Attitudes,* 2nd ed. (Belmont, CA: Wadsworth, 1981).
2. Albert Mehrabian, personal website, www.kaaj.com/psych/smorder.html. Quoted by permission.
3. W. Chalmers Brothers, Jr., *Language and the Pursuit of Happiness* (Naples, FL: New Possibilities Press, 2005).
4. Malcolm Gladwell, *Blink: The Power of Thinking Without Thinking* (New York: Little, Brown, 2005), pp. 197–221, 208.
5. Kristi Hedges, "The Leadership Factor: The Language of Action, Part I," Copyright 2009 by *Entrepreneur.com* Inc. All rights reserved.
6. Uri Hasson and Scott Berinato, "I Can Make Your Brain Look Like Mine," *Harvard Business Review,* December 1, 2010, pp. 32–33.

Chapter 3: Stopping the Negativity Loop

1. Martin E. P. Seligman, Ph.D., *Learned Optimism: How to Change Your Mind and Your Life* (New York: Pocket Books, 1998); and Martin E. P. Seligman, Ph.D., *Authentic Happiness* (New York: Free Press, 2002).
2. Martin E. P. Seligman, Ph.D., *The Optimistic Child* (New York: Houghton Mifflin, 1995).
3. Office of Applied Studies, Results from the 2004 National Survey on Drug Use and Health: National Findings, DHHS Publication No. SMA 05-4062, NSDUH Series

H-28 (Rockville, MD: Substance Abuse and Mental Health Services Administration, 2005).

4. Marcus Buckingham and Donald O. Clifton, Ph.D., *Now, Discover Your Strengths* (New York: Free Press, 2001).

5. Belle Linda Halpern and Kathy Lubar, *Leadership Presence* (New York: Gotham Books, 2003), p. 35.

Chapter 4: Presence as Perception

1. Material in this story is derived from Ted Leonsis with John Buckley, *The Business of Happiness: 6 Secrets to Extraordinary Success in Life and Work* (Washington, D.C.: Regnery Publishing, 2010); and Kristi Hedges, "The Leadership Factor: The Business of Happiness," *Entrepreneur.com*, August 2010.

Chapter 5: Go Ahead, Trip Over Your Own Perfectionism

1. Robert I. Sutton, "How to Be a Good Boss in a Bad Economy," *Harvard Business Review*, June 2009.

Chapter 6: Trust: The Ultimate Gatekeeper

1. Gallup research as cited in Marcus Buckingham and Curt Coffman, *First, Break All the Rules: What the World's Greatest Managers Do Differently* (New York: Simon & Schuster, 1999), p. 32.

2. David H. Maister, Charles H. Green, and Robert M. Galford, *The Trusted Advisor* (New York: First Touchstone, 2000).

3. Robert Rosenthal, Ph.D. and Lenore Jacobson, Ed.D., *Pygmalion in the Classroom* (New York: Holt, Rinehart and Winston, 1968).

4. Susan Scott, *Fierce Conversations* (New York: Berkley Trade, 2004), pp. 5–6.

Chapter 7: What You Can Learn About Emotional Intelligence While Riding in the Elevator

1. Peter Salovey and John D. Mayer, "Emotional Intelligence," *Imagination, Cognition, and Personality* 9 (1990), pp. 185–211.

2. Daniel Goleman, *Emotional Intelligence* (New York: Bantam Books, 1996); and Daniel Goleman, *Working with Emotional Intelligence* (New York: Bantam Books, 1998).

3. Steven J. Stein, Ph.D. and Howard E. Book, M.D., *The EQ Edge* (Mississauga, ON: John Wiley & Sons, 2006).

4. Tony Hsieh, interview by Adam Bryant, "On a Scale of 1 to 10, How Weird Are You?" *New York Times*, January 9, 2010.

5. See Peter F. Drucker, *Management: Tasks, Responsibilities, Practices* (New York: Harper & Row, 1973); Stephen R. Covey, *The 7 Habits of Highly Effective People* (New York: Fireside Books, 1989); James M. Kouzes and Barry Z. Posner, *The Leadership Challenge* (San Francisco: Jossey-Bass, 2002); and Peter M. Senge, *The Fifth Discipline: The Art and Practice of the Learning Organization* (New York: Currency/Doubleday, 2006).

6. Belle Linda Halpern and Kathy Lubar, *Leadership Presence* (New York: Gotham Books, 2003), p. 109.

7. Covey, *7 Habits of Highly Effective People,* p. 235.
8. Christopher Twarowski and Frank Ahrens, "Workers Shaken by Fannie, Freddie Woes," *Washington Post,* July 14, 2008.
9. Chris Segall, personal interview with author, February 3, 2011.

Chapter 9: Inspiring Change from the Brain Down

1. David Rock, *Quiet Leadership* (New York: Harper Collins, 2006); David Rock, *Your Brain at Work* (New York: Harper Business, 2009); and personal interview with author, November 4, 2010.
2. Daniel Pink, *Drive* (New York: Riverhead, 2009).
3. Marshall Goldsmith, *What Got You Here Won't Get You There* (New York: Hyperion, 2007), p. 14.
4. Mark H. Histed, Anitha Pasupathy, and Earl K. Miller, "Learning Substrates in the Primate Prefrontal Cortex and Striatum: Sustained Activity Related to Successful Actions," *Neuron* 63, no. 2 (July 2009), pp. 244–253; and Edward M. Hallowell, "Managing Yourself: What Brain Science Tells Us About How to Excel," *Harvard Business Review,* December 2010.
5. Mihaly Csikszentmihalyi, *Flow* (New York: Harper Perennial Modern Classics, 2008).
6. Daniel Pink, personal interview with author, November 8, 2010.
7. For more information on neuroscience, especially as applied to management decision making and the workplace, see Dan Ariely, *Predictably Irrational* (New York: Harper Collins, 2009); Jonah Lehrer, *How We Decide* (New York: First Mariner Books, 2009); and Read Montague, *Your Brain Is (Almost) Perfect: How We Make Decisions* (New York: Plume, 2006).

Chapter 10: From Vision to Visionary

1. Jonah Lehrer, *How We Decide* (New York: First Mariner Books, 2009).
2. Jim Collins, *Good to Great* (New York: Harper Collins, 2001).
3. Tony Hsieh, *Delivering Happiness: A Path to Profits, Passion, and Purpose* (New York: Business Plus, 2010).
4. Peter M. Senge, *The Fifth Discipline: The Art and Practice of the Learning Organization* (New York: Currency/Doubleday, 2006).
5. Kristi Hedges, "The Leadership Factor," *Entrepreneur.com,* March 2009; and Niki Leondakis, personal interview with author, February 17, 2009.

Chapter 12: Strategic Shock Value and Other Ways to Create Shining Moments

1. Robert I. Sutton, "How to Be a Good Boss in a Bad Economy," *Harvard Business Review,* June 2009.
2. Keith Ferrazzi, *Never Eat Alone* (New York: Currency Doubleday, 2005).

Appendix: Quick Hit I-Presence Tips

1. U.S. Bureau of Labor Statistics, *American Time Use Survey,* news release, June 22, 2010.

Index

accountability, 35–36
acknowledgment
  agreement vs., 123
  in DIAL in process, 171
  and empathy, 123, 205
actions, 23
  aligning intentions with, 23
  aligning thoughts with, 10
  micro- vs. macro-, 24
  and personal presence brand, 36–40
  vs. talk, 39–40
  trust in, 34
  of visionary, 172–173
adolescents, depression diagnoses, 45
agenda for meetings, 193
agreement, vs. acknowledgment, 123
Aha! moments, 144, 147
  acting on, 151–152
  time for developing, 168
Allison, Herb, 126
American Time Use Study (U. S. Bureau
  of Labor Statistics), 220
analyzing phase of thought, 144
anger, and sending email, 134
anomie, 162
Apple brand, 16
appreciative inquiry technique, 150
approachability, 75–76
Association for Financial Professionals,
  113
athlete, visualization by, 11

attention
  focus on what's right, 45
  focused, 147–148
  paying, 40–41
"attention density," 148, 151
attire, *see* clothes (dress)
attitudes, superior, 117
audit, *see* personal presence audit
authenticity, 9, 190, 210
  in actions, 24
  in connections, 75
automatic responses, 144
autonomy trigger, in threat-reward
  response, 156

bad news, email and, 133
Bar-On, Reuven, 109
BarOn EQ-i test (Emotional
  Quotient Inventory), 109, 115,
  120
blame, accepting responsibility for, 36
blazer, 28
Blink (Gladwell), 31–32
boards of directors, and CEO perfection-
  ists, 80–81
body language, 2, 24–29
  as contagious, 32–33
  researching, 30
  thoughts and, 29
  see also actions
boss, qualities of great, 77–78

About the Author

Kristi Hedges is a serial entrepreneur, communications expert, and sought-after leadership coach. In her 20-year career working with leaders to help them communicate more effectively, she's encountered every personality type imaginable, yet remains more than a little passionate that anyone can learn presence. Her workshops and coaching programs have been used by CEOs and teams in organizations from the Fortune 10 to the U.S. government to nonprofits. She runs her own coaching practice, The Hedges Company, and is a founding partner in the leadership development firm, Element North.

Kristi writes about leadership for Forbes.com and is regularly featured in publications such as *The Wall Street Journal, The Financial Times, Entrepreneur, BBC, Chief Learning Officer* and *CNBC*. She's been honored as one of the "50 Women Who Mean Business in Washington, D.C." and as an owner of a top 25 Largest Women-Owned Businesses by the *Washington Business Journal*. She is a frequent keynote speaker for organizations and events around the world.

Prior to becoming a leadership coach, Kristi co-founded and ran one of the first technology communications firms in the Washington, D.C. area for a decade before successfully selling her interest. Her career highlights also include working for a national news outlet, and as a political consultant for dozens of electoral campaigns from U.S. President to statewide offices. Kristi holds a B.A. from Virginia Tech and an M.S. from Purdue University, both in communications.

She is an ICF-credentialed leadership coach through Georgetown University, and is a teaching faculty member of the Georgetown University Institute for Transformational Leadership. Kristi lives in suburban Washington, D.C. with her husband and two children.

For additional resources, to stay in touch, and for more information about Kristi's executive coaching, keynotes, group workshops, or I-Presence training, please visit:

Web: thehedgescompany.com
Blog: kristihedges.com
Facebook: facebook.com/powerofpresence
Twitter: @kristihedges

9 780814 437858